A NATURALIST'S G

BIRDS
OF
SRI LANKA

Gehan de Silva Wijeyeratne

JOHN BEAUFOY PUBLISHING

This edition published in the United Kingdom in 2020 by John Beaufoy Publishing Ltd
11 Blenheim Court, 316 Woodstock Road, Oxford OX2 7NS, England
www.johnbeaufoy.com

10 9 8 7 6 5 4 3 2 1

Photo Captions and credits
Front cover: *main image* Female Sri Lanka Green-pigeon © Namal Kamalgoda; *bottom left* Grey-capped Emerald Dove © Namal Kamalgoda; *bottom centre* Chestnut-backed Owlet © Namal Kamalgoda; *bottom right* Greater Coucal © Ajith Ratnayaka. **Back cover:** Golden-fronted Leafbird © Gehan Rajeev
Title page: Scarlet Minivet © Gehan Rajeev **Contents page**: Caspian Tern © Gehan de Silva Wijeyeratne

Main descriptions: photos are denoted by a page number followed by t (top), b (bottom), l (left), c (centre) or r (right).
Mohammed Abidally 96t; **Atul Dhamankar** 52t; **Keith Dover** 82b; **Athula Edirisinghe** 154t; **Graham Ekins** 31b; **Con Foley** 83bl, 83br; **Matt Jones** 41b; **Namal Kamalgoda** 83t, 88tl, 88tr, 93bl, 93br, 102tl, 102tr, 116tr, 128b, 129tl, 133tl, 140tl, 140tr, 146bl, 146br; **Udaya Karunaratne** 61b, 78t, 79bl, 81tl, 81tr, 90tl, 90tr; **Chamindha A Mahanayakage** 142b, 143bl; **Manjula Mathur** 67b, 68tl; **Brian Mellows** 68tr; **Doug Radford** 90b; **Gehan Rajeev** 38t, 39b, 47tl, 47tr, 63tl, 63tr, 91bl, 91br, 92b, 100t, 103bl, 103br, 105b, 110br, 112b, 117bl, 117br, 121t, 126t, 132br, 152tr, 156bl, 156br; **Ajith Ratnayake** 21tl, 21tr, 73b, 85b, 103tl, 103tr, 107t, 148t, 155tl, 157bl, 157bc, 157br; **Dr Sumit Sengupta** 33t; **Tom Tams** 31t; **Cherry Wong** 53b, 54t; **Peter and Michelle Wong** 33b.

Gehan de Silva Wijeyeratne is happy to receive images as additions or as replacements for images in his photographic field guides to birds, butterflies and dragonflies, mammals, wild flowers and trees. For more details contact him on gehan.desilva.w@gmail.com

ISBN 978-1-913679-00-2

Edited by Krystyna Mayer
Designed by Gulmohur Press
Printed and bound in Malaysia by Times Offset (M) Sdn. Bhd.

·CONTENTS·

ACKNOWLEDGEMENTS

GENERAL

Many people have over the years helped me to become better acquainted with the natural history of Sri Lanka. My field work has also been supported by several tourism companies as well as state agencies and their staff. To all of them, I am grateful. I must, however, make a special mention of the corporate and field staff of Jetwing Eco Holidays, and its sister companies Jetwing Hotels and Jetwing Travels. During my 11 years of residence in Sri Lanka they hugely supported my efforts to draw attention to Sri Lanka as being super-rich in wildlife. The following past and present staff who have helped in numerous ways include Chandrika Maelge, Amila Salgado, Ajanthan Shantiratnam, Paramie Perera, Nadeeshani Attanayake, Ganganath Weerasinghe, Riaz Cader, Ayanthi Samarajewa, Shehani Seneviratne, Aruni Hewage, Divya Martyn, L. S. de S Gunasekera, Chadraguptha Wickremesekera ('Wicky'), Supurna Hettiarachchi ('Hetti'), Chaminda Jayaweera , Sam Caseer, Chandra Jayawardana, Nadeera Weerasinghe, Anoma Alagiyawadu, Hasantha Lokugamage 'Basha', Wijaya Bandara, Suranga Wewegedara, Prashantha Paranagama, Nilantha Kodithuwakku, Dithya Angammana, Asitha Jayaratne, Lal de Silva, Hiran Cooray, Shiromal Cooray, Ruan Samarasinha, Raju Arasaratnam, Sanjiva Gautamadasa and Lalin de Mel, and interns.

My late Uncle Dodwell de Silva took me on Leopard safaris at the age of three and got me interested in birds. My late Aunt Vijitha de Silva and my sister Manouri got me my first cameras. My late parents Lakshmi and Dalton provided a lot of encouragement; perhaps they saw this as a good way of keeping me out of trouble. My sisters Indira, Manouri, Janani, Rukshan, Dileeni and Yasmin, and brother Suraj also encouraged my pursuit of natural history. In the UK my sister Indira and her family always provided a home when I was bridging islands. Dushy and Marnie Ranetunge helped me greatly on my return to the UK and indirectly supported my natural history writing. My one-time neighbour Azly Nazeem, a group of then schoolboys including Jeevan William, Senaka Jayasuriya and Lester Perera, and my former scout master Mr Lokanathan were key influences in my school days.

My development as a writer is owed to many people. Firstly my mother Lakshmi and more lately various editors who encouraged me to write. A bird book such as this inevitably draws on childhood inspiration from books that were available then, and G. M. Henry and W. W. A. Phillips, whom I never met, armed me with the literature I needed as a teenage birder. I was also inspired by the work in *Loris* by photographers such as Dr T. S. U. de Zylva and Lal Anthonis, and by the programme of events organized by the WNPS, FOGSL and SLNHS. The late Thilo Hoffman of the Ceylon Bird Club and Professor Kotagama have been inspirations, with their tireless work in bird conservation.

My wife Nirma and daughters Maya and Amali are also a part of the team. Their contribution is not always obvious in the finished product, but their support and encouragement is very strong. They put up with me not spending the time they deserve from me because I spend my private time working on the 'next book'. Nirma, at times with help from parents Roland and Neela Silva, takes care of many things, allowing me more time to spend on taking natural history to a wider audience.

The list of people and organizations who have helped or influenced me is too long to mention individually and the people mentioned here are only representative. My apologies to those whom I have not mentioned by name; your support did matter.

SPECIFIC

Tara Wikramanayake helped enormously with much useful feedback and copy-edited early drafts of the text. Tara Wikramanayake, Kithsiri Gunawardana and Dr Pathmanath Samaraweera provided useful comments in updating the checklist of the birds of Sri Lanka for the first edition. Any responsibility for errors in ascribing a status remains mine. Many years ago Avanti Wadugodapitiya helped to 'fit' into a standard structure species text I had written, which I have used in this book. Both John Beaufoy and Rosemary Wilkinson were gently persistent that I should embark on another book with them. I once again benefitted from Krystyna Mayer, an experienced natural history editor, who performed the final edit.

Introduction

This book does not cover all the bird species recorded in Sri Lanka. It does, however, feature the majority of the most common birds, including around 90 per cent of the species that will be seen by casual birdwatchers (only a few rare migrants and vagrants are included), and is thus useful as a starter book.

The text on the birds is aimed primarily at eliminating some of the confusion that may arise in identification in the field because of varying plumages of the same species, or confusion with similar-looking species.

The majority of the birds in the book were photographed in Sri Lanka by the author. Where images taken outside Sri Lanka have been used, these species or subspecies are not diagnosably different in the field for the purpose of identification. Pictures contributed by other photographers are individually credited (see p. 2).

Bird Calls & Songs

Calls and songs are very important in separating bird species, and brief descriptions are given for the birds that are vocal. A bird can have a range of vocalizations depending on its age and sex, and any interspecific and intraspecific interactions. Representative calls are described here, although it is always a struggle to transcribe vocalizations and everyone has their own method of doing so.

Voice descriptions are given only for birds that are generally vocal, and where the vocalizations are useful in field identification. For some species the vocalizations are *the* crucial clue to recording their presence or absence at a site. Other birds, such as some waterbirds and seabirds, tend to be generally quiet – many of them do utter grunts and squawks occasionally, for example at nesting colonies, but these have virtually no value in field identification. Descriptions of their voices are therefore not included.

CDs with the songs and calls of Sri Lankan birds have been produced by Deepal Warakagoda and a few other sound recordists. These are useful for birdwatchers who wish to develop their fieldcraft further. There are also many resources on the Internet for learning bird calls. One of the best is www.xeno-canto.org, which was one of the references used to complement the author's own sound recordings, as was http://avocet.zoology.msu. edu. The best way to learn the vocalizations is to listen carefully in the field, then refresh your memory by listening to recordings.

PLUMAGE

In some species adult males and females have different plumages, as for the Common Teal shown below. In all birds juveniles are different from adults. However, from the viewpoint of identification for birders this is usually only important in the case of birds such as gulls, which may take 2–4 years to attain their adult plumage. Many northern-latitude species that winter in Sri Lanka have marked differences between their summer (or breeding) and winter (non-breeding) plumages. In resident Sri Lankan birds a change can at times be observed between breeding and non-breeding plumages. However, the change is not as dramatic and is most common in waterbirds, in which the bare parts can take on bright colours.

Male Common Teal

Female Common Teal

Birdwatching in Sri Lanka

Below is a brief overview of birdwatching highlights in Sri Lanka.

- There are 34 endemic bird species – a very high density of endemics given the size of the country.
- Birds are surprisingly tame whether they are in a national park or in an urban setting. Many bird photographers remark on how easy it is to take pictures of the birds. Even birds that are familiar worldwide, such as many waders, present better photographic opportunities in Sri Lanka than they do in other parts of the world.
- On the moderately sized island that is Sri Lanka, the birding sites are highly varied, including lush lowland rainforests, cloud forests, elephant- and Leopard-rich dry lowlands, wetlands and coastlines.
- The roads and accommodation infrastructure are good, and there is a mature tourist industry with English spoken widely in cities and even in remote areas.
- There are a number of specialized wildlife and birding tour companies catering for both local and foreign birders.
- A good variety of natural history publications on Sri Lanka is available for reference.

Black-headed Ibis and Asian Openbills in Talangama Wetland

TOP SITES

For visiting foreign birders the key targets are the endemics that are found in the wet zone. To find these it is essential to visit a good lowland rainforest site such as Sinharaja and a montane site such as Horton Plains National Park. Birders in search of the endemics should also fit in Kithulgala Rainforest to maximize their chances, and a visit to a national park such as Yala is recommended. The following are the main sites visited by birders on two-week tours to Sri Lanka.

Sinharaja Rainforest

Lowland Wet Zone	
Talangama Wetland	In Colombo's suburbs, visited on arrival or before departure. Good range of wetland birds, often at close quarters.
Bodhinagala	Optional. Small but rich patch of rainforest about 1½ hours from Colombo.
Sinharaja	The most important site. All but a handful of endemic birds can be seen here.
Morapitiya	Optional. Morapitiya on the way to Sinharaja can at times be rewarding. Check the state of the access road, as this is highly variable.
Kithulgala	Rainforest in the mid-hills that has the mix of bird species found in Sinharaja. Essential second stop for those wanting to see all the endemics.
Montane Zone	
Horton Plains National Park	This, together with sites such as Hakgala Botanical Gardens, is essential for some of the montane endemics such as the Ceylon Whistling-thrush.
Dry Lowlands (South)	
Yala, Bundala, Palatupana	Yala and Uda Walawe are excellent for a variety of dry-zone birds. Yala is also a good place to see Leopards, Asian Elephants and Sloth Bears; Uda Walawe for elephants. Bundala National Park and Palatupana Salt Pans afford good views of migrant waders and other such birds.
Dry Lowlands (North-central)	
Mannar Island	Migrant waders, waterfowl, gulls and Deccan Plateau residents rare or absent further south. Generally of more interest to resident birders.

Yala National Park

Horton Plains National Park

Bodhinagala Rainforest

Knuckles Range

Minneriya National Park

Sinharaja

Urani River East Coast

Wilpattu National Park

ENDEMIC BIRDS

At present 34 bird species are recognized as being endemic to Sri Lanka. These are listed below in their family groups for convenience, as they are often targets for visiting birders.

Partridges, Quails & Pheasants, Phasianidae

Sri Lanka Spurfowl *Galloperdix bicalcarata*

Sri Lanka Junglefowl *Gallus lafayetii*

Pigeons and Doves, Columbidae

Sri Lanka Woodpigeon
Columba torringtoniae

Sri Lanka Green-pigeon *Treron pompadora*

Parrots, Psittacidae

Sri Lanka Hanging-parrot
Loriculus beryllinus

Layard's Parakeet *Psittacula calthropae*

Cuckoos, Cuculidae

Green-billed Coucal
Centropus chlororhynchos

Red-faced Malkoha
Phaenicophaeus pyrrhocephalus

Owls, Strigidae

Serendib Scops-owl *Otus thilohoffmanni*

Chestnut-backed Owlet
Glaucidium castanonotum

Hornbills, Bucerotidae
Sri Lanka Grey Hornbill *Ocyceros
gingalensis*

Barbets, Capitonidae

Yellow-fronted Barbet *Psilopogon flavifrons*

Sri Lanka Small Barbet *Psilopogon rubricapillus*

Woodpeckers, Picidae

Lesser Sri Lanka Flameback
Dinopium psarodes

Greater Sri Lanka Flameback
Chrysocolaptes stricklandi

Swallows & Martins, Hirundinidae

Cuckooshrikes, Campephagidae

Sri Lanka Swallow *Hirundo hyperythra*

Sri Lanka Woodshrike *Tephrodornis affinis*

Bulbuls, Pycnonotidae

Black-capped Bulbul
Pycnonotus melanicterus

Yellow-eared Bulbul
Pycnonotus penicillatus

Thrushes, Turdidae

Spot-winged Thrush
Geokichla spiloptera

Sri Lanka Scaly Thrush
Geokichla imbricata

Sri Lanka Whistling-thrush
Myophonus blighi

Babblers, Timaliidae

Ashy-headed
Laughingthrush
Garrulax cinereifrons

Brown-capped Babbler
Pellorneum fuscocapillus

Sri Lanka Scimitar Babbler
*Pomatorhinus [schisticeps]
melanurus*

Babblers,
Timaliidae

Old World Warblers,
Sylviidae

Flowerpeckers,
Dicaeidae

Sri Lanka Rufous Babbler
Turdoides rufescens

Sri Lanka Bush-warbler
Elaphrornis palliseri

Legge's Flowerpecker
Dicaeum vincens

White-eyes, Zosteropidae

Old World Flycatchers & Chats, Muscicapidae

Sri Lanka Hill White-eye *Zosterops ceylonensis*

Dusky Blue Flycatcher *Eumyias sordidus*

Starlings & Mynas, Sturnidae

White-faced Starling *Sturnornis albofrontatus*

Sri Lanka Hill-myna *Gracula ptilogenys*

Drongos, Dicruridae

Sri Lanka Crested Drongo *Dicrurus lophorinus*

Crows, Jays, Magpies & Treepies, Corvidae

Sri Lanka Blue Magpie *Urocissa ornata*

Bird Orders & Families

As many as 471 bird species have been recorded in Sri Lanka at the time of writing. The table below compares the number of orders and families based on the *HBW and Birdlife International Illustrated Checklist of the Birds of the World* with what is found in Sri Lanka. The number of genera and bird species in the world are based on the IOC World Bird List v 10.1. Sri Lanka has a surprisingly high proportion of birds at the level of orders (c. ⅔) and families (c. ⅓). Furthermore, on average, almost one in every two birds is in a different genus.

	World	Sri Lanka	%
Orders	36	23	64%
Families	243	87	36%
Genera	2,322	265	11%
Species	10,929	471	4%
Average number of species per genus	4.7	1.8	

Residents & Migrants

The number of species found as Migrants only just about exceed species which occur only as Residents. Five per cent of species are found as both Residents and Migrants, which means that these species will have a resident subspecies (or race) as well as a subspecies that migrates to Sri Lanka.

	No.	%
Resident	216	46%
Migrant	229	49%
Resident and migrant	26	5%
	471	100%

HOW MANY BIRDS CAN YOU SEE?

Of the 471 species recorded in Sri Lanka, 18 occur only as Highly Scarce Migrants and 109 occur only as Vagrants; a total of 127. This leaves 344 species as Residents and Migrants. A few of these Residents and Migrants are rare. If we therefore take 90 per cent of this number, we get approximately 310 species. Thus if a person who lives in Sri Lanka or is a regular visitor to the island has seen 300 species in the country, this is a good 'country list'.

For birders on a dedicated birding tour seeing anything in excess of 200 species is good, and seeing 235 would make for a very good trip list. What is special for visiting birders is the 34 endemics, as well as the ease of viewing many species at close range.

STATUS

The status of birds given in this book was derived and updated from *A Pictorial Guide and Checklist of the Birds of Sri Lanka* by Gehan de Silva Wijeyeratne (2007). The abbreviations for status in the species accounts are a combination of letters indicating a measure of abundance (for example common, uncommon, scarce), and their status with respect to whether they are resident or migrant. The measure of abundance is subjective in the absence of quantitative data. It is based on field experience going back many years, and published information that takes into account both the geographical spread and the number of birds. Should the Square-tailed Black Bulbul, which is a highly conspicuous bird in well-visited wet-zone forests like Sinharaja, be treated as a common resident (CR) or merely as a resident (R)? On an island-wide basis it would be better to describe it as an uncommon resident (UR), as it is largely confined to wet-zone areas, preferably with good forest stands. Similarly, Lesser Sand Plovers, although seen in large numbers, are listed as migrants (M) rather than common migrants (CM), because they are confined to relatively small areas of suitable habitat.

In this book the key used for the island-wide status of birds is as follows.

Abundance		Resident/Visitor
C Common		R Resident
U Uncommon		M Migrant
S Scarce		E Endemic
H Highly, as in highly scarce (HS)		V Vagrant

For birds that have a threat category in relation to the IUCN Red List of Threatened Species, this is quoted. References to the IUCN Red List are to the list of 2007.

D. P. Wijesinghe's *Checklist of the Birds of Sri Lanka* (1994) is used as the basis for the subspecies. Any doubt about the identity of a subspecies is indicated by a question mark. Some birds occur as both resident subspecies and migrant subspecies. This is indicated by the presence of more than one status.

VAGRANT OR HIGHLY SCARCE MIGRANT?

A bird that is classified as a vagrant to Sri Lanka is a bird that is not normally expected to occur as a winter or passage visitor. Such birds may only be recorded a few times in a decade or even a century. Some vagrants have been recorded only once.

A highly scarce migrant is a bird that is expected to occur in Sri Lanka regularly, but in such small numbers that in some years it may not occur at all; or its presence may fail to be recorded due to an absence of observers, or limited access by observers to areas where the species is likely to be seen.

In the case of some birds, such as the Blue-and-White Flycatcher, establishing its status as a Vagrant is easy. It winters in Southeast Asia and there is only one record of it in South Asia; a recent record from Sri Lanka. There are other birds, such as waders and seabirds like petrels, which at the time of recording may have had only one record or a few records. However, with more observers and increasingly high skill levels among them, and as more people are going out on pelagic trips, some of these birds may have their status revised to Highly Scarce Migrants, Scarce Migrants or Uncommon Migrants.

This list is conservative and treats species as Vagrants if the records are few in number. But with more and better quality observer effort in the future, the statuses could change. At present of the birds recorded in Sri Lanka, 18 are treated as only Highly Scarce Migrants and 109 as Vagrants. Where a bird has more than one subspecies occurring in Sri Lanka, its status is treated as that of the most abundant subspecies.

The following 18 species are Highly Scarce Migrants: Rain Quail, African Comb Duck, Oriental Turtle-dove, Baillon's Crake, Barau's Petrel, Lesser Frigatebird, Great Frigatebird, Christmas Frigatebird, Great Knot, Eurasian Woodcock, Jack Snipe, Lesser Noddy, Sandwich Tern, Parasitic Skua, Long-legged Buzzard, Eurasian Wryneck, Amur Falcon and Citrine Wagtail.

The following 109 species are Vagrants: Greylag Goose, Bar-headed Goose, Ruddy Shelduck, Ferruginous Duck, Tufted Duck, Gadwall, Lesser Flamingo, Pale-capped Pigeon, Red Turtle-dove, Great Eared-nightjar, Himalayan Swiftlet, Pacific Swift, Asian Emerald Cuckoo, Indian Water Rail, Corn Crake, White-faced Storm-Petrel, Black-bellied Storm-Petrel, Cape Petrel, Bulwer's Petrel, Jouanin's Petrel, Streaked Shearwater, Sooty Shearwater, Short-tailed Shearwater, Black Stork, White Stork, Goliath Heron, Chinese Pond Heron, Schrenk's Bittern, Eurasian Bittern, Red-footed Booby, Oriental Plover, Grey-headed Lapwing, Sociable Plover, Red Knot, Red-necked Stint, Sharp-tailed Sandpiper, Pectoral Sandpiper, Dunlin, Spoon-billed Sandpiper, Buff-breasted Sandpiper, Asian Dowitcher, Wood Snipe, Swinhoe's Snipe, Great Snipe, Spotted Redshank, Small Buttonquail, Sooty Gull, Steppe Gull, Slender-billed Gull, Black-naped Tern, White-cheeked Tern, South Polar Skua, Long-tailed Skua, Black Baza, European Honey-buzzard, Egyptian Vulture, Pied Harrier, Eurasian Sparrowhawk, Tawny Eagle, Bonelli's Eagle, Greater Spotted Eagle, European Roller, Lesser Kestrel, Red-headed Falcon, Eurasian Hobby, Oriental Hobby, Black-naped Oriole, Bay-backed Shrike, Great Grey Shrike, Greater Short-toed Lark, Black-browed Reed-warbler, Booted Warbler, Lanceolated Warbler, Common Grasshopper Warbler, Indian Broad-tailed Grass-warbler, Dusky Crag-martin, Wire-tailed Swallow, Streak-throated Swallow, Northern House-martin, Dusky Warbler, Western Crowned Warbler, Lesser Whitethroat, 'Desert' Whitethroat, Chestnut-tailed or Grey-headed Starling, Daurian Starling, Common Starling, Eyebrowed Thrush, Rufous-tailed Scrub-robin, Spotted Flycatcher, Blue-and-White Flycatcher, Blue-throated Flycatcher, Bluethroat, Yellow-rumped Flycatcher, Rufous-tailed Rock-thrush, Whinchat, Siberian Stonechat, Pied Wheatear, Desert Wheatear, Isabelline Wheatear, Asian Fairy-bluebird, Chestnut-shouldered Bush-sparrow, White-browed Wagtail, Tawny Pipit, Olive-backed Pipit, Red-throated Pipit, Common Rosefinch, Black-headed Bunting, Red-headed Bunting and Grey-necked Bunting.

Bird Topography

To get to grips with identifying birds, it is very useful to learn the topographical terms for the parts and plumage areas of a bird. The following terms for birds' body parts are often used throughout the text.

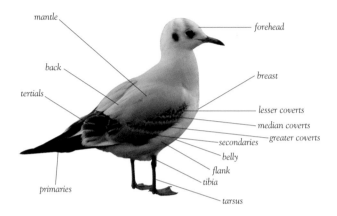

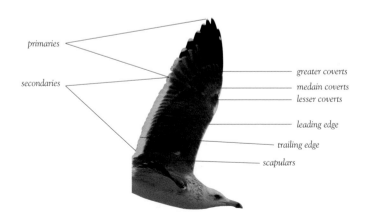

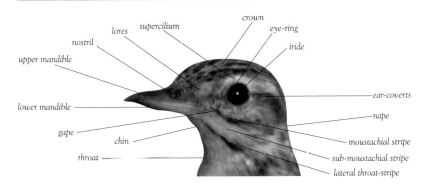

Glossary

Axillaries Feathers in 'armpit' of a bird, that is at base of underwing.
Heterodactyl Third and fourth toes face forwards; first and second toes face backwards. Only characteristic in trogons.
Onomatopoeic Name of bird is derived from its call; for example, call of Chiffchaff sounds like 'chiff chaff'.
Remiges Primary and secondary flight feathers.
Zygodactyl Second and third toes face forwards; first and fourth toes face backwards, as in woodpeckers and cuckoos.
Kleptoparasitism Usually refers to bird of one species stealing food from another. May also refer to stealing nest material.

Species Accounts

Identifying birds becomes easier once you gain familiarity with general bird types. Scientists group all species into genera, which are in turn grouped into families, in turn grouped into orders. The tree of life attempts to clarify the inter-relationship of all living beings in the animal and plant kingdoms. The various ways in which scientists try to classify animals and plants is the science of taxonomy and is outside the scope of this book. However, controversy and debate rage on how best to do this and as a result, perhaps in the case of birds in particular, different books frequently classify species differently.

The common name of a bird is followed by its scientific name, which generally has two parts, the genus and the specific epithet. No two species can have the same scientific binomial, these names are relatively stable and a species should have only one accepted scientific name at any given time. Common names, on the other hand, can vary considerably from one country or region to another. In cases where birds are described as subspecies (or geographical races), they have trinomials.

Endemics are identified with the symbol ⓔ beside the scientific name.

Indian Peafowl ■ *Pavo cristatus*

DESCRIPTION Head and neck of male in breeding plumage iridescent, glossy peacock-blue. Male grows train of feathers during breeding season, and dances with tail feathers

raised to form a fan with shimmering eyes. Outside breeding season male sheds the train. He retains black-and-white barred wings and scapular feathers, whereas female's are brown with pale edges. **HABITAT** Dry-zone scrub jungle. **DISTRIBUTION** Mainly dry lowlands, although found in a few wet-zone areas that border dry lowlands. **VOICE** Honk followed by loud, double-noted, trumpeting call that rises slightly in pitch. Sounds mournful. **STATUS** R.

LEFT: *Male*, RIGHT: *Female*

Grey Francolin ■ *Francolinus pondicerianus pondicerianus*

DESCRIPTION Pale sandy-brown overall; wings with chequered pattern in muted

browns. Fowl-sized, and confusion is unlikely with much smaller quails. Oval throat-patch yellow with distinct edges. **HABITAT** Dry scrub. **DISTRIBUTION** Dry lowlands in area north of Puttalam, extending to the Jaffna Peninsula. It is curious that such a gregarious bird has not spread to suitable habitats in the south. **VOICE** Metallic, loud, double-noted call that is repeated. **STATUS** UR.

Sri Lanka Spurfowl ■ *Galloperdix bicalcarata*

DESCRIPTION Male boldly spangled with white edged with black; large, teardrop-shaped markings on wings. Red facial patch duller in female, which is dull brown overall. Always seen in pairs; does not form flocks. **HABITAT** Appears to need densely shaded or riverine forests. **DISTRIBUTION** Found wherever there are decent-sized patches of wet-zone forests, from lowlands to highlands. In dry zone found along riverine forests. **VOICE** Fortunately it is very vocal, as it is heard often but hardly ever seen. Series of ascending calls that begin as yelping notes and change into high-pitched *chuk chuk* notes. Sequence broken by interspersal of differently pitched notes. Voice complex, varied and unmistakable. **STATUS** UE.

Female   *Male*

Sri Lanka Junglefowl ■ *Gallus lafayetii*

DESCRIPTION Female brown with barred wings. Yellow patch in middle of comb distinguishes male from domestic cockerel. Neck and mantle golden. **HABITAT** Appears to survive only where sizeable tracts of protected areas remain. This could be an effect of hunting, and the birds are very shy outside national parks. **DISTRIBUTION** Widespread up to mountains wherever large tracts of forest survive. Dry zone seems to be the stronghold. **VOICE** Call a tremulous *churro-choik churro-choik* with an incredulous sounding intonation. **STATUS** CE.

LEFT: *Female*, RIGHT: *Male*

Lesser Whistling-duck ▪ *Dendrocygna javanica*

DESCRIPTION Confusion possible between this species and vagrant **Fulvous Whistling Duck** *Dendrocygna bicolor*. Latter has white-streaked flanks, off-white upper-tail coverts

and black line on upper side of neck. Lesser has chestnut wing-coverts that contrast with dark flight feathers. Fulvous has uniformly dark upper wings. **HABITAT** Marshes and lakes in lowlands. Bird of fresh water; does not use brackish waterbodies. Feeds on aquatic vegetation. **DISTRIBUTION** Common throughout lowlands, ascending to mid-hills. **VOICE** Also known as Whistling Teal on account of whistling calls, usually uttered in flight. Heard quite often in flight at night. **STATUS** R.

Cotton Teal
▪ *Nettapus coromandelianus*

DESCRIPTION Diminutive duck. Male has green back, white neck and head with dark crown, and black collar. Female brown and white with dark line through eye. Male has prominent white wing-bar, lacking in female. Females always have one or more males associating with them. **HABITAT** Water-lily covered lakes in lowlands. **DISTRIBUTION** Seems most common in dry lowlands. **STATUS** UR.

Male

Eurasian Wigeon ▪ *Anas penelope*

DESCRIPTION Male has conspicuous white forewings. In eclipse plumage he looks like female, without a buff crown. In breeding plumage male develops delicate pink on breast that contrasts subtly with light grey flanks and back. Horizontal white line may show on inner secondaries. **HABITAT** Winter visitor to coastal wetlands. **DISTRIBUTION** Very rare in south, but flocks of several hundred are seen in northern coastal wetlands. **VOICE** Males utter clear, whistled *whee oh*. **STATUS** M.

Male   *Female*

Indian Spot-billed Duck ▪ *Anas poecilorhyncha poecilorhyncha*

DESCRIPTION Large size, yellow band towards tip of grey-black bill, scalloped sides and upperparts, and heavy spotting on breast. Green speculum bordered by thin white wing-bar in front and thick white patch formed by tertials show well in flight. Sexes similar, with male having larger red loral patch than female. **HABITAT** Freshwater bodies. **DISTRIBUTION** Around Mannar and the Northern Peninsula. Mannar remains the best place to see this rare bird in Sri Lanka. **STATUS** HSR, SM. Formerly considered a scarce winter migrant. Young were observed in 2003 in Talladi Ponds, near Mannar Causeway. This suggests that it could be a breeding resident in these areas. Classified as Highly Endangered on IUCN Red List.

Common Teal ■ *Anas crecca crecca*

DESCRIPTION Small duck easily overlooked in mixed duck flocks. Male has chestnut head and green eye-patch. In eclipse plumage looks like drabber female. Male has spotting on breast. **HABITAT** Coastal wetlands. **DISTRIBUTION** Most likely to be seen in northern wetlands around Mannar and Jaffna, where individuals may be encountered in mixed duck flocks. Other likely locations include Bundala in south. **VOICE** High-pitched, whistled note spaced at short intervals. **STATUS** SM.

Male

Female

Northern Pintail ■ *Anas acuta acuta*

DESCRIPTION In non-breeding plumage male similar to female, but retains grey on upper wing. Lead-grey bill distinguishes nondescript female from other ducks. In breeding plumage male develops chocolate-brown hood with thin white finger running up along neck; 'pin tail' also develops. **HABITAT** Large flocks often occupy waterbodies, both fresh and brackish, in lowlands. **DISTRIBUTION** Winter visitor in large numbers to coastal wetlands in south (for example Bundala) and strip from Mannar to the Northern Peninsula. **VOICE** A few varied calls; whistled *kloop* at rest. **STATUS** M.

Male

Female

Garganey ▪ *Spatula querquedula*

DESCRIPTION In non-breeding plumage male similar to female, but retains bluish-grey on upper wing. In breeding plumage male acquires prominent white eyebrow. Rare migrant **Gadwall** *S. strepera* has orange in bill and white patch on inner secondaries. **HABITAT** Freshwater lakes in lowlands, especially dry lowlands. Seems equally at home in freshwater bodies and brackish water. **DISTRIBUTION** Common migrant to freshwater wetlands in dry lowlands; less common in wet lowlands. May also be seen in brackish water, but this is not its preferred habitat. **VOICE** A few varied calls; one rapid honking call. **STATUS** M. Abundant winter visitor.

Female

Northern Shoveler ▪ *Anas clypeata*

DESCRIPTION In non-breeding plumage male similar to female, but retains pale blue on upper wing, and has darker belly than female. Female's flanks buff with thick dark brown (brown looks black) tips to feathers, creating scaly pattern. Feathers on upperparts dark, with pale edges creating scaly effect. Pattern on male is different, although this is not shown well in many field guides. Sieves water by rapidly moving bill from side to side while swimming. Often a flock of birds whirls around together. Upends occasionally. **HABITAT** Coastal wetlands. **DISTRIBUTION** In south, around Mannar and the Northern Peninsula. **VOICE** Punchy, sibilant honk, rapidly repeated. **STATUS** SM.

Male

Female

Little Grebe ■ *Tachybaptus ruficollis capensis*

DESCRIPTION In breeding plumage neck and cheeks turn deep chestnut. Crown and upper half of face turn black. Gape develops pale patch that can look luminescent green at close range. In non-breeding plumage colours are duller. Sexes similar. **HABITAT** Lowland freshwater lakes. Common bird in aquatic habitats, but easily overlooked because of its small size and discreet habits. At times teams of Little Grebes gather to form rafts

that may hold over a hundred birds; lakes in Annaiwilundawa are a good site to see this phenomenon. **DISTRIBUTION** Widespread in lowlands. Scarce in hills, although present on Lake Gregory in Nuwara Eliya in highlands. **VOICE** Whinnying call that is heard most frequently during breeding season. **STATUS** R.

Breeding

Greater Flamingo ■ *Phoenicopterus roseus*

DESCRIPTION Looks quite plain when scarlet-and-black wings are tucked beneath pale

mantle. **HABITAT** Salt pans and lagoons in coastal areas. Filter feeder, consuming tiny aquatic animals and micro-organisms. **DISTRIBUTION** At present occurs mainly around Hambantota, Mannar Causeway and the Northern Peninsula. No confirmed records of breeding in Sri Lanka, although birds have constructed nest mounds and abandoned them. Their movements between India and Sri Lanka are not regular, and there can be a gap of a few years when they are absent. Migrants to Sri Lanka believed to breed in the Rann of Kutch. **VOICE** Flock keeps up continuous babble of goose-like honking noises. **STATUS** M.

Sri Lanka Woodpigeon
■ *Columba torringtoniae* ℮

DESCRIPTION Bluish-grey body with black-and-white pattern on purplish hindneck. Distinctly larger than a feral pigeon. **HABITAT** Large forested stretches in highlands. Seasonal movements to lower hills, descending as low as Sinharaja. **DISTRIBUTION** Horton Plains National Park and botanical gardens in Hakgala are two of the most reliable sites for it. Main walking trail of Sinharaja from Kudawa side is seasonally good – when birds are present they are tolerant of observers. **VOICE** Deep, throaty *whoo*, with an owl-like quality. **STATUS** UE.

Western Spotted Dove ■ *Spilopelia suratensis*

DESCRIPTION Bold hindneck marking that is spangled with black and white. Mantle feathers have dark bases, and wing-coverts have dark shaft streaks towards tips. All of this creates a mottled pattern on upperparts. **HABITAT** Tolerant of human presence. **DISTRIBUTION** Widespread throughout Sri Lanka. One of the most common birds in dry lowlands. Since the late 1990s has been spreading into wet zone. By 2000 it had colonized Colombo, where it can now be heard cooing in the mornings. Expansion in range may be related to climate change. **VOICE** Throaty and tremulous *kuk kuk krooo* repeated many times. **STATUS** CR.

Eurasian Collared-dove ■ *Streptopelia decaocto*

DESCRIPTION Plain dove with black hind-collar. Can easily be separated from more common Western Spotted Dove (see p. 27), which is patterned on wings with

chequerboard pattern on hind-collar. **HABITAT** Mainly northern dry lowlands. **DISTRIBUTION** Northern parts of Sri Lanka. Southern limit around Nawadamkulama Tank; Deccan plateau species with restricted distribution in Sri Lanka. Mannar a good site for it. **VOICE** Archetypical *whoo whoo whooo* cooing call of a dove. Notes often sound like *cu-ckoo*. **STATUS** UR.

Grey-capped Emerald Dove ■ *Chalcophaps indica*

DESCRIPTION A fast-flying dash of green across a road in a national park is often how the Emerald Dove is seen. In Sinharaja, where these ground-feeding doves are habituated,

it is possible to see them feeding on the ground. Small size, emerald-green wings and black-and-white barred back make the species distinctive. White supercilium less clear-cut in female than in male. **HABITAT** Occupies remnant patches of forest. Seems to need densely shaded forests and has all but disappeared from environs of Colombo, although occasionally seen in suburbs around the Talangama Wetland. **DISTRIBUTION** Throughout Sri Lanka. **VOICE** Repeated *oom oom*. Birders are always surprised that this booming call originates from a tiny pigeon. **STATUS** R.

Orange-breasted Green-pigeon ■ *Treron bicinctus leggei*

DESCRIPTION Both sexes have grey hindnecks; these are greenish in Sri Lanka Green-pigeon (see below). Under-tail coverts of latter also heavily marked with green. **HABITAT** Forested areas in lowlands. **DISTRIBUTION** Large flocks sometimes gather in dry-zone scrub forests. **VOICE** Undulating whistle with chirruping notes interspersed. Has a musical quality to it and notes are complex, with variations uttered in different pitches. Similar to Sri Lanka, sings with theme of whistled *ooo we ooo we oooo*, but song is sharper and has quivering notes at the end of a whistle reminiscent of a motorcycle that has been kick-started. **STATUS** R.

LEFT: *Female*, RIGHT: *Male*

Sri Lanka Green-pigeon ■ *Treron pompadora* ⓔ

DESCRIPTION Male has conspicuous purple mantle which female lacks. Female similar to Orange-breasted Green-pigeon (see above); most easily told apart by greenish rather than grey nape. Under-tail coverts also help to distinguish females: yellow in Sri Lanka and cinnamon-red on inner webs of Orange-breasted. **HABITAT** Similar to Orange-breasted's, but less common. **DISTRIBUTION** Throughout Sri Lanka. **VOICE** Call a whistled *ooo we ooo we oooo* repeated with variations. **STATUS** E.

Male

Green Imperial-pigeon
■ *Ducula aenea pusilla*

DESCRIPTION Largest species of pigeon resident in Sri Lanka. Green upperparts. **HABITAT** Areas with tall forest. Favours canopies of tall trees. Diet mainly fruits, which are swallowed whole; hard seed is disgorged. **DISTRIBUTION** Throughout Sri Lanka, except far north. Visits Talangama Wetland near Colombo to feed on fruiting trees. Strong flier that may cover large distances in a day. **VOICE** Deep, throaty *room room room* booming from canopy; sometimes escalates to *oop oop oop* call. **STATUS** R.

Ceylon Frogmouth ■ *Batrachostomus moniliger*

DESCRIPTION Female always rufous. Male occurs in grey and brown colour phases

(morphs). Male identified by pale, 'lichen-like' patches on lower scapulars and tertials. **HABITAT** Well-forested areas in lowlands. **DISTRIBUTION** Widespread in lowlands where remnant patches of forest are found. May occupy degraded habitats, but only if they adjoin good-quality forest. Subcontinental endemic found in India in the Western Ghats. **VOICE** Harsh, explosive *whaa* descending in tone. **STATUS** R.

LEFT: *Male*, RIGHT: *Female*

Jerdon's Nightjar ■ *Caprimulgus atripennis aequabilis*

DESCRIPTION Male has single white bar on throat similar to Indian Little Nightjar's (see below). Female lacks white spot. Both Jerdon's and Indian Little have mantle feathers with pale edges; greater coverts also have pale edges, giving rise to wing-bars. Jerdon's a little more contrastingly plumaged than Indian Little, and has longer tail. Jerdon's also appreciably larger than Indian Little (size of Yellow-billed Babbler, (see p. 136). Size and call may be best features to refer to for distinguishing the species from each other. **HABITAT** Resident of dry lowlands, especially in areas of open scrub. Often calls from perch used as vantage point on tree or bush. **DISTRIBUTION** Mainly dry zone from lowlands to mid-hills. A few populations in wet zone. Several birds have been recorded in wet zone during migrant season, getting lost and going into houses, including in Colombo. It is possible that there might be a 'local movement', or possibly an influx of migratory birds. **VOICE** Quivering, double-noted *ku-krr*, with a liquid quality. **STATUS** R.

Indian Little Nightjar ■ *Caprimulgus asiaticus eidos*

DESCRIPTION Similar to Jerdon's Nightjar; see details under Jerdon's (above). Indian Little smaller – approximately the size of Red-vented Bulbul (see p. 129). Indian Little has strongly streaked crown (Jerdon's also streaked) and buff hindneck-patch. White throat-bar broken in middle (Jerdon's unbroken). Central-tail feathers unmarked (marked in Jerdon's). **HABITAT** Open areas in dry lowlands. **DISTRIBUTION** Mainly dry zone from lowlands to mid-hills. A few populations in wet zone. **VOICE** *Chuk chuk chukoor* with the last note tremulous. Has been likened to sound of marble being dropped. An onomatopoeic name for this bird is Marble Dropper. **STATUS** R.

Crested Treeswift ■ *Hemiprocne coronata*

DESCRIPTION Overall impression is of large, grey, swift-like bird with long wings and long tail. Not as highly manoeuvrable in the air as a swift, and perches frequently on branches. Male's ear-coverts red; female's dark grey, almost black. Both sexes have tall crest at base of beak; crest raised when bird is perched. **HABITAT** Widespread in lowlands and lower hills. Most likely to be encountered close to forest patches. **DISTRIBUTION** Widespread except in highlands. Absent from urban areas. **VOICE** Nasal, double-note *kee-yeew*, usually uttered on the wing. **STATUS** R.

LEFT: *Female*, RIGHT: *Male*

Male

Indian Swiftlet ■ *Aerodramus unicolor*

DESCRIPTION Plain colour separates this species from Little Swift (see p. 33), which has a white rump. Shorter tail separates it from Asian Palm Swift (see p. 33). Indian has distinctive flight, gliding with wings stiffly held parallel to the ground. Glides last only a few seconds and are interspersed with rapid fluttering of wings. Previously known as Indian Edible-nest Swiftlet. **HABITAT** Generally found not far from good-quality forests, although can sometimes nest in urban environments. **DISTRIBUTION** Wet zone, ascending to highlands. **VOICE** High-pitched, chittering calls. Sounds very similar to Little Swift. **STATUS** R.

Asian Palm-swift
■ *Cypsiurus balasiensis balasiensis*

DESCRIPTION May be confused with Indian Swiftlet (see opposite). Distinguished from that species by its comparatively long wings and long tail. Tail sporadically spread open, showing fork. Overall impression is of greyish-brown bird. **HABITAT** Most common in lowlands up to mid-hills. A flock may move around, but is 'centred' around a grove of palm trees most of the time. **DISTRIBUTION** Widespread throughout Sri Lanka. **VOICE** Brief chittering call, high in pitch, uttered frequently as a flock swoops around. **STATUS** R.

Little Swift
■ *Apus affinis singalensis*

DESCRIPTION White rump against black plumage distinctive (previously known as White-rumped Swift). White throat may not show in flight. Underparts often look plain black, and general impression is of overall black swift until white rump is seen. **HABITAT** Usually near rocky outcrops, where it nests in caves or overhangs. May nest in old buildings. **DISTRIBUTION** Occurs in large flocks throughout Sri Lanka up to mid-hills. **VOICE** High-pitched, loud, screeching call uttered on the wing as it careers around. **STATUS** R.

Green-billed Coucal
■ *Centropus chlororhynchos* ℮

DESCRIPTION Looks very similar to Greater Coucal (see below). Green rather than black bill diagnostic. Wings duller, and not bright chestnut as in Greater. Black on body glossier. **HABITAT** Restricted to good-quality rainforests of large extent. Its survival in the relatively tiny Bodhinagala Rainforest is an anomaly – it may be lost from this reserve within the next few decades as urbanization continues. **DISTRIBUTION** Restricted to a few lowland rainforests such as Sinharaja, Morapitiya and Kithulgala. A few also live in small pockets such as Bodhinagala. **VOICE** Call a *whoop-whoop whoop-whoop whoop-whoop*, or could even be transcribed as a *whoo whoo*. Softer sounding than that of common Greater. **STATUS** HSE. Probably one of Sri Lanka's most endangered birds.

Greater Coucal ■ *Centropus parroti*

DESCRIPTION Black bird with stern red eyes and chestnut wings. Old name of Crow Pheasant captures its appearance and habits well. Previously known as Greater Coucal,

a name now reserved for a species found in northern India. **HABITAT** Variety of habitats from forest to disturbed areas in urban gardens. Often feeds on the ground. In urban habitats feeds on snails; presence of invasive Giant African Snail *Lissachatina fulica* may be a key factor to it thriving in urban gardens. **DISTRIBUTION** Widespread. **VOICE** Broad range of vocalizations. Rapid and forceful *oop oop oop*. Some scolding calls. Throaty *kok* uttered at times. **STATUS** CR.

Sirkeer Malkoha ▪ *Taccocua leschenaultii leschenaultii*

DESCRIPTION Plain brown, long-tailed malkoha with prominent red bill. **HABITAT** Lowland scrub jungle adjoining grassland. Often seen foraging on the ground. **DISTRIBUTION** Dry lowlands in south-east Sri Lanka. Appears to have very specific habitat requirements. In Yala National Park, for instance, it can be seen in very specific locations, unlike Blue-faced Malkoha (see p. 36), which can show up almost anywhere. **VOICE** Metallic *pip* that sounds like two pebbles being struck together. **STATUS** UR.

Red-faced Malkoha ▪ *Phaenicophaeus pyrrhocephalus* ℮

DESCRIPTION Male has brown irides; female's are pale. **HABITAT** Bird of tall rainforests. In the 18th century it was recorded by Captain Legge in Kotte on the outskirts of Colombo, which indicates how rapid deforestation was in the 19th century. Mainly insectivorous, but opportunistically feeds on ripe berries.
DISTRIBUTION Confined to a few remaining tall forests in lowland rainforests. Sinharaja, Morapitiya and Kithulgala are reliable for sightings. **VOICE** Generally silent, but occasionally utters a guttural rattling call; almost a croak. **STATUS** SE. Classified as Vulnerable on IUCN Red List.

Male　　　　　　　　　　　*Female*

Blue-faced Malkoha ▪ *Phaenicophaeus viridirostris*

DESCRIPTION In flight white edges on long tail show up. **HABITAT** Generally a shy bird of lowland scrub jungle. Feeds on a variety of plant and animal matter, including Maliththan *Salvadora persica* fruits. Most of diet probably consists of insects. **DISTRIBUTION** Dry lowlands. **VOICE** Like most malkoha species does not vocalize strongly, at times uttering a soft guttural call in flight. **STATUS** UR.

Jacobin Cuckoo
▪ *Clamator jacobinus jacobinus*

DESCRIPTION Adult, black-and-white birds unmistakable. Juveniles look like browner versions of adults. In flight they show white wing-patches. **HABITAT** Forested areas in lowlands. Most likely to be seen in scrub jungle in dry lowlands. Where it occurs in wet zone, found in wetlands close to mangrove thickets. **DISTRIBUTION** Widespread from lowlands to mid-hills. **VOICE** Repetitive, metallic piping call. **STATUS** UR.

Western Koel ■ *Eudynamys scolopaceus scolopaceus*

DESCRIPTION Male looks similar to a crow in glossy black plumage. However, ivory-coloured bill, red eyes and slimmer shape distinguish it from crows. Female brown, heavily barred and spotted with white. **HABITAT** Favours lightly wooded areas with fruiting trees. Frequents gardens in cities. Very partial to fruits of palms and ripening papayas. **DISTRIBUTION** Throughout Sri Lanka. **VOICE** Series of *ko wuu* calls. About 7–8 notes usually uttered very loudly, each rising in pitch and sounding more insistent. Notes can change as they become somewhat tremulous. May also rapidly utter three *ko wuu kowuu ko wuu* notes of even pitch. Sinhala name *Koha* somewhat onomatopoeic and derived from these *ko wuu* notes. Can also produce a cackle of a few *kik kik* notes. The author once observed a male calling for at least half an hour on and off, while another male was perched less than a metre away. **STATUS** CR.

LEFT: *Female*, RIGHT: *Male*

Grey-bellied Cuckoo ■ *Cacomantis passerinus*

DESCRIPTION Adult male is grey. Female also has a brick-red (or hepatic) form. In grey-phase birds white edge on shoulder can be a useful field characteristic at times. Tail can look pointed or squarish. Previously also known as Plaintive Cuckoo, a name now reserved for *Cacomantis merulinus* found in Southeast Asia, which migrates to India but is not recorded in Sri Lanka. Change of name causes some confusion, as older literature uses the name Plaintive Cuckoo. **HABITAT** Most likely to be seen in areas of scrub forest. **DISTRIBUTION** Widespread winter visitor to dry-zone scrub forests, but also found in wet zone and lower hills. **VOICE** Repeated, whistled *tcheow*. **STATUS** M.

LEFT: *Hepatic form female*, RIGHT: *Male*

Slaty-legged Crake ■ *Rallina eurizonoides amauroptera*

DESCRIPTION Slaty legs, ruddy breast and grey beak. Slaty-breasted Rail (see below) also has slaty legs, but breast is slaty and upperparts are barred. Black-and-white barring on underparts of Slaty-legged sharper and more contrasting. Upperparts dark brown with no barring. Juveniles similar, but juvenile Slaty-breasted Rail has darker breast and neck, and unbarred upperparts. Juveniles of both species have pale chins. **HABITAT** Marshes and damp thickets. **DISTRIBUTION** Can be seen on arrival anywhere in Sri Lanka. Most records appear to be in wet zone and within that in highlands. This observation may, however, be due to observer bias as the birding circuit focuses on the wet zone. **VOICE** Repeated *onk onk* with nasal twang. **STATUS** UM, HSR. One record of bird with chicks.

Slaty-breasted Rail ■ *Lewinia striatus*

DESCRIPTION Slaty legs (see also Slaty-legged Crake, above). Slaty breast can look bluish. Pale reddish beak distinguishes this species from Slaty-legged Crake, but confusion is possible with vagrant **Water Rail** *Rallus aquaticus*, which has a red bill. Water Rail does not have barred upperparts. Juveniles barred above. **HABITAT** Marshy areas and paddy fields. Skulks in cover. **DISTRIBUTION** Resident throughout Sri Lanka, but often overlooked due to discreet habits. Resident population supplemented in winter by migrants. **VOICE** Frog-like *blip* note, repeated frequently. **STATUS** UR, UM.

White-breasted Waterhen ■ *Amaurornis phoenicurus phoenicurus*

DESCRIPTION Prominent white face and breast, and slaty upperparts. Young covered in black down. **HABITAT** Wetlands, canals, ditches and other such areas, in lowlands and mid-hills.

DISTRIBUTION Widespread throughout Sri Lanka. No patch of marsh, even in suburban areas, appears to be without a pair of these birds. **VOICE** Pair may engage in some noisy duetting, with call *korawak korawak* repeated at length. Sinhala name of '*Korawakka*' is onomatopoeic. **STATUS** CR.

Watercock ■ *Gallicrex cinerea cinerea*

DESCRIPTION Breeding male dark (almost black) overall, with red 'plate' on upper mandible. Non-breeding male and female similar pale brown overall. Upperparts scaly, with pale edges to dark-centred feathers. **HABITAT** Secretive bird of lowland marshes. Tends to emerge into the open in the evening, although may also be seen in the afternoon heat walking across water-lily covered lakes. **DISTRIBUTION** Widespread throughout lowlands. Prefers marshes bordered by dense vegetation. Talangama Wetland is a regular site for birders. **VOICE** Repeated soft and liquid-like, sharp *ooh*. **STATUS** UR.

Purple Swamphen ▪ *Porphyrio poliocephalus poliocephalus*

DESCRIPTION Large rail with red legs and bill, and blue body. Juveniles grey and downy. Sexes similar. **HABITAT** Common in freshwater marshlands in lowlands. Males highly

combative during breeding season and frequent clashes take place between them. Feeds largely on aquatic plant material. **DISTRIBUTION** Throughout lowlands. Most common in dry zone as a result of large number of open waterbodies located there. **VOICE** Grating calls, metallic trilling calls. Also nasal *wah wah* calls like a tired animal exhaling breath. **STATUS** R.

Common Moorhen ▪ *Gallinula chloropus indica*

DESCRIPTION Overall dark-looking bird, on closer inspection with brownish wings and dark underparts. White jagged line on sides shows as horizontal line when bird is floating

in water in duck-like fashion. Yellow-tipped bill with red base and forehead plate. Dark underparts distinguish it from White-breasted Waterhen (see p. 39). Shorter legged than Watercock (see p. 39), which lacks white line. **HABITAT** Freshwater bodies in lowlands. **DISTRIBUTION** Throughout lowlands. Not particularly common anywhere. **VOICE** A few croaking notes. **STATUS** R.

Wedge-tailed Shearwater ■ *Ardenna pacifica*

DESCRIPTION Like Flesh-footed Shearwater (see below), this bird has flesh-coloured feet. Its more slender, all-dark bill is the best feature that separates it from Flesh-footed.

Wedge tail does not always show well. Bill pattern the best field characteristic. Also longer necked than Flesh-footed, but this is not always apparent. **HABITAT** Pelagic. **DISTRIBUTION** Arrives in around mid-April before south-west monsoon. Sightings peter out by end of April, when seas become too rough for birders to go out in a boat. **STATUS** M

Flesh-footed Shearwater ■ *Ardenna carneipes*

DESCRIPTION Tail shorter and more rounded than that of Wedge-tailed Shearwater (see above). Legs and feet pink, but not diagnostic as this characteristic is shared with Wedge-tailed. Stout pink bill with dark tip the best field characteristic. In flight in good light, primaries are supposed to show pale patch. **HABITAT** Pelagic. **DISTRIBUTION** Arrives just before south-west monsoon in around early to mid-April. Conditions are too rough to go out to sea on the west coast from late April, so there is an absence of records after this time. **STATUS** M.

Persian Shearwater ■ *Puffinus persicus*

DESCRIPTION Pale underparts and brown upperparts. Bill grey with darker tip. In April 2010 a flock of 35 Persian Shearwaters was sighted. **HABITAT** Pelagic. **DISTRIBUTION** Appears to arrive in around mid-April before south-west monsoon. Sightings peter out by end of April, when seas become too rough for birders to go out to sea. Photographs taken in April 2010 off Kalpitiya were probably the first high-quality photographs taken in Sri Lankan waters as these birds are rarely seen. As increasing numbers of birdwatchers hire boats to run north–south transects between the E 79 35 and E 79 38 lines of longitude, many hitherto scarcely seen pelagics such as this species will probably be seen and photographed more frequently. **STATUS** SM.

Painted Stork

■ *Mycteria leucocephala*

DESCRIPTION Yellow bill, orange face, and black-and-white body with pink flush on rear end. Bill slightly curved down at tip. **HABITAT** Mainly edges of open waterbodies. Also wades into centres of shallow ponds. **DISTRIBUTION** Dry lowlands. Birds in wet zone originate from colony in Colombo Zoo. **STATUS** R.

Asian Openbill

■ *Anastomus oscitans*

DESCRIPTION Black-and-white plumage; superficially similar to vagrant **White Stork** *Ciconia ciconia* in body-plumage pattern, but bill thick with gap between mandibles (the 'open bill'). This characteristic is only clear at close range. Bill colour a dirty white. **HABITAT** Marshes, paddy fields, and edges of lakes and ponds. **DISTRIBUTION** Mainly lowlands, but ascends up to mid-hills. **STATUS** R.

Woolly-necked Stork ■ *Ciconia episcopus episcopus*

DESCRIPTION Black with white neck and under-tail coverts. Black plumage has glossy sheen. **HABITAT** Meadows and grassland not far from water. Diet based more on terrestrial animals than aquatic ones. **DISTRIBUTION** Confined to dry lowlands. **STATUS** R.

Black-necked Stork ■ *Ephippiorhynchus asiaticus asiaticus*

LEFT: *Male*, RIGHT: *Female*

DESCRIPTION Large stork with black neck and black-and-white body. Male has brown irides; female has yellow ones. **HABITAT** Lagoons and adjoining grassland. Seldom seen in fresh water. **DISTRIBUTION** Largely confined to dry lowlands in south. In May 2011 one was recorded in Trincomalee – a record for this bird in the north-east after a lapse of 50 years. A few birds present in areas of Yala and Kumana. Over the years number of individuals known from south has never increased to more than half a dozen or so. **STATUS** HSR.

Lesser Adjutant ■ *Leptoptilos javanicus*

DESCRIPTION Large stork with grey plumage, yellow bill and naked yellow neck. **HABITAT** Grassland never far from water. Often seen feeding on small terrestrial animals like frogs and reptiles, as are other storks, but also known to scavenge on dead animals. **DISTRIBUTION** Dry lowlands. **STATUS** SR. Rare outside protected areas. Globally endangered species classified as Vulnerable on IUCN Red List.

Glossy Ibis ■ *Plegadis falcinellus falcinellus*

DESCRIPTION The only all-dark species of ibis in Sri Lanka. **HABITAT** Freshwater wetlands and mangrove areas. **DISTRIBUTION** Can turn up anywhere in lowlands, from wetlands such as Talangama close to Colombo, to wetlands in dry lowlands such as Kalametiya. Small flocks of up to half a dozen have been recorded. The birds seem to move a lot. **STATUS** SM, HSR. Breeding observed in 2020.

Black-headed Ibis ■ *Threskiornis melanocephalus*

DESCRIPTION Black head and neck, and white body. Downcurved bill. **HABITAT** Marshes and wet fields in lowlands. Often feeds in paddy fields when they have just been ploughed or have lain fallow. Prey composition varies from soil-dwelling invertebrates to small vertebrates and invertebrates on dry soils. Interestingly, G. M. Henry describes it as largely nocturnal, although the author has never thought of it as such. **DISTRIBUTION** Widespread in lowlands ascending to mid-hills. **STATUS** R.

Eurasian Spoonbill ■ *Platalea leucorodia leucorodia*

DESCRIPTION Buffy-yellow breast-band in breeding plumage. During breeding season develops crest of feathers on back of head. Dark bill tipped yellow. **HABITAT** Lagoons and freshwater bodies in dry lowlands. Eats a wide range of animals, including amphibians and insects. **DISTRIBUTION** Wide distribution: found across Europe, Africa and Asia. **STATUS** UR.

Little Egret ■ *Egretta garzetta garzetta*

DESCRIPTION Bill black and 'pencil thin', and yellow on feet always separates this species from other egrets. At peak of breeding season feet and lores turn flesh coloured, and breeding birds develop 'aigrette' plumes. **HABITAT** Widespread, mainly in lowlands. Occurs on almost any waterbody from lagoons and rivers to canals, in fresh- and brackish-water habitats. Also gathers at freshly ploughed paddy fields. **DISTRIBUTION** Mainly lowlands, but ascends up to mid-hills and most common in dry lowlands. **VOICE** As in all egrets vocabulary limited to a few guttural calls. **STATUS** CR.

Breeding

Western Reef-egret ■ *Egretta gularis schistacea*

DESCRIPTION Occurs in dark and white morphs as well as in intermediate forms. Grey morph grey all over with white chin. Note that Little Egret (see opposite) can also have a grey morph. Best field characteristic is bill, which is heavier than that of Little. Also yellow on feet in reef-heron usually extends up to tibia, sometimes as far up as hock joint. However, some Little Egrets have yellow extending up feet beyond 'yellow slippers'. **HABITAT** Coastlines and lagoons. **DISTRIBUTION** Coastal wetlands, but rare in southern half of Sri Lanka. Most records are from Mannar and in strip extending north from Kalpitiya. **STATUS** SM.

Great Egret ■ *Ardea alba*

DESCRIPTION Separated from Intermediate Egret (see p. 48) by gape line, which extends behind eye. Largest of the egrets. Yellow bill turns black in breeding plumage. At peak of breeding season lores turn blue and tibia turns crimson. **HABITAT** Large waterbodies and marshes in lowlands. **DISTRIBUTION** Common in lowlands; ascends up to mid-hills. **VOICE** In flight often utters a low croak. Sometimes this is voiced as a protest; at other times it is a contact call. **STATUS** CR.

Breeding

Intermediate Egret ▪ *Ardea intermedia intermedia*

DESCRIPTION In breeding plumage yellow bill turns black with a dusky tip. Separated from Little Egret (see p. 46) by heavier bill and black feet. Smaller than Great Egret (see p. 47) and larger than Little. **HABITAT** Freshwater sites. **DISTRIBUTION** Especially dry zone. **STATUS** CR.

Grey Heron ▪ *Ardea cinerea cinerea*

DESCRIPTION About the size of Purple Heron (see opposite). Grey wings; white neck and head with black side-stripe on crown. Briefly during breeding season legs turn crimson, beak becomes orange and birds develop plumes. **HABITAT** Lowland lakes and marshes. Comfortable in stretches of open water. Feeds on a variety of aquatic animals. **DISTRIBUTION** Dry zone. **VOICE** Harsh, loud *kraa* calls usually in flight. **STATUS** R.

Breeding

Purple Heron
■ *Ardea purpurea manilensis*

DESCRIPTION Rufous on neck with greyer body and wings. Considerably larger, vagrant **Goliath Heron** *Ardea goliath* has heavy grey bill. Purple's bill is yellow. Plumage and bill colours brightest in breeding adults. **HABITAT** Lowland lakes and marshes. Equally at home in swampy habitats in dry and wet zones. Prefers areas of reed bed. **DISTRIBUTION** Mainly wet-zone lowlands and less frequently dry lowlands, where it feeds on a variety of aquatic animals. **VOICE** Guttural *kreek* in flight; rolling series of guttural calls when interacting. **STATUS** R.

Cattle Egret ■ *Bubulcus ibis*

DESCRIPTION Heavy jowl (puffy throat) and stocky build separate this species from other egrets. Golden-buff wash on head, neck, face and breast in breeding plumage. Legs black in both breeding and non-breeding birds. **HABITAT** Mainly lowland paddy fields and grassy pastures. Increasingly seen at refuse dumps. **DISTRIBUTION** Throughout Sri Lanka. In the 2000s it began to spread to highlands. Ambewala Cattle Farm near Horton Plains may be a factor in helping it to establish around Horton Plains National Park. Climate change could be another factor. **STATUS** CR.

Breeding

Indian Pond Heron ■ *Ardeola grayii grayii*

DESCRIPTION Streaked brown upperparts make this bird vanish in grassy environments. When it suddenly takes flight, its clean white wings are visible. During breeding season

fleshy parts change colour. Lores turn bluish, legs turn crimson, especially around hock joint, and mantle turns purple. Bill black tipped with yellow in breeding and non-breeding birds. Vagrant **Chinese Pond Heron** *Ardeola bacchus* has grey back, but in non-breeding plumage species are hard to separate. **HABITAT** Marshes, paddy fields and even cricket grounds in lowlands. **DISTRIBUTION** Widespread across Sri Lanka up to highlands. **VOICE** Usually silent; utters a protesting *kreek* when flushed. **STATUS** CR. Possibly the most abundant wetland bird.

Striated (Little Green) Heron ■ *Butorides striata javanicus*

DESCRIPTION Dark crown contrasts with grey upperparts. Wing feathers pale edged, giving scalloped effect. Juveniles brown, with white spots on tips of coverts forming bars, and with streaks

underneath. **HABITAT** Brackish swamps and mangroves in lowland wetlands. **DISTRIBUTION** Throughout coastal lowlands; seems to be most common in coastal mangroves from Kalpitiya to Mannar. **VOICE** Usually silent; flies away with a staccato alarm call when disturbed. **STATUS** UR.

Black-crowned Night-heron ■ *Nycticorax nycticorax nycticorax*

DESCRIPTION Juveniles brown spotted with white. Fleshy parts change colour at peak of breeding. Males develop fine nuchal crest and their legs turn crimson. **HABITAT** Thickets in low-lying lakes. Not confined to freshwater habitats and can be seen in brackish habitats as well, although freshwater lakes and rivers seem to be its preferred habitat. **DISTRIBUTION** Throughout lowlands to mid-hills. Its presence may be overlooked on account of its nocturnal habits. **VOICE** Often utters a harsh guttural *kwok* call, betraying its presence when flying overhead. **STATUS** UR.

Yellow Bittern

■ *Ixobrychus sinensis*

DESCRIPTION Juveniles streakier than adults. Contrasting upper wing that shows clearly in flight. Similar Chestnut Bittern (see p. 52) lacks black flight feathers. **HABITAT** Swamps and marshes in lowlands. **DISTRIBUTION** Uncommon breeding resident in lowlands. Migrant birds spread all over Sri Lanka up to mid-hills. Commonly seen during winter. **STATUS** UR, M. The most common of the four bitterns found in Sri Lanka, with a resident race as well as a migrant one.

Chestnut Bitter

■ *Ixobrychus cinnamomeus*

DESCRIPTION Uniform chestnut-brown upper wing separates this species from Yellow Bittern (see p. 51), which has black flight feathers. **HABITAT** Freshwater marshes and lakes with dense aquatic vegetation. **DISTRIBUTION** Scarce breeding resident in lowlands; even more rare up to mid-hills. **STATUS** UR.

Black Bittern ■ *Ixobrychus flavicollis*

DESCRIPTION Black overall with thick yellow stripe on sides of neck and thinner pale stripes on front of body running from chin to breast. Female duller than male, a brownish-black. Juveniles like paler females with pale edges to wing feathers. **HABITAT** Swamps and marshes in lowlands; occasionally forested streams. **DISTRIBUTION** Rare breeding resident in lowlands. Migrant birds spread all over Sri Lanka up to mid-hills. Talangama Wetland a reliable site for birders. **VOICE** Sounds like a frog barking. **STATUS** UR, M.

Spot-billed Pelican ■ *Pelecanus philippensis*

DESCRIPTION Duck-like gait in the water and an enormous bill. Spots on bill can be seen at close quarters. Flight feathers show only slight contrast with white wing lining on underwing. **Great**

White Pelican *Pelecanus onocrotalus*, with which it has been confused, has black flight feathers that contrast strongly on underwing. **HABITAT** Larger lakes in dry lowlands. Occasionally may scoop up fish in flight when water levels are low. More commonly seen fishing on the water in groups. **DISTRIBUTION** Bird of dry zone. Birds seen in wet zone originate from population in Colombo Zoo. **STATUS** R.

Christmas Frigatebird ■ *Fregata andrewsi*

DESCRIPTION Adult males easy to identify as they are all dark underneath except for white belly-patch near vent.

Female has white belly with pair of broad white strips extending out to wings, and another pair of white strips extending out to sides of head. Immature females also show this pattern of white belly fastened onto underwing and neck with white strips, but the contrast is less. Careful examination of photographs is needed to distinguish immatures of this species from those of **Lesser Frigatebird** *Fregata ariel*. **HABITAT** Pelagic. **DISTRIBUTION** Bad weather may bring birds close to shore during south-west monsoon (May–July). **STATUS** HSM.

Female

53

Brown Booby ■ *Sula leucogaster plotus*

DESCRIPTION Adult Brown Booby shows dark wing edges underneath and brown, not white, on upper breast, distinguishing it from juvenile **Masked Booby** *Sula dactylatra*. Masked has white hind-collar. **HABITAT** Pelagic. **DISTRIBUTION** Sri Lanka is visited by birds that breed on Indian Ocean islands. Occasional records from seabird roosts on rocky islands on south-west coast. Also recorded off Kalpitiya. Potentially may turn up anywhere on coastline. **STATUS** SM.

Breeding

Little Cormorant
■ *Microcarbo niger*

DESCRIPTION Bill the best field characteristic separating this species from Indian Cormorant (see opposite). Bill short and stubby in Little, slender and long in Indian. Juveniles brown with white throats. Their underparts turn scaly before they assume adult plumage. During the breeding season, a little tuft of white feathers develops on the ear-coverts, which can be seen in the picture. In the man-made lakes in the dry zone, Little Cormorants can gather in flocks numbering several hundred. **HABITAT** Freshwater lakes and rivers in lowlands. **DISTRIBUTION** Throughout Sri Lanka, but numbers greatest in dry lowlands. **STATUS** CR.

Indian Cormorant or Shag ▪ *Phalacrocorax fuscicollis*

DESCRIPTION Relatively long and slender bill. Bluish eyes. Juveniles brown with white throats. There is a little white ear-tuft in breeding plumage. At close quarters birds also show greenish irides. **HABITAT** Freshwater lakes and rivers in lowlands, preferring lakes to rivers and streams. At times flocks of hundreds can gather to hunt fish. **DISTRIBUTION** Throughout Sri Lanka but numbers are greatest in dry lowlands. **STATUS** CR. Not as abundant as Little Cormorant (see opposite).

Great Cormorant ▪ *Phalacrocorax carbo sinensis*

DESCRIPTION Breeding adults have white flank-patches. In addition to pale area around bill, feathers on crown and on face surrounding bare skin around bill turn white. Thick crescent of black behind eye remains, providing a contrast. Birds look white headed from a distance. White edging continues on back of head and along neck. Patch of orange-coloured, bare facial skin below eyes with blue irides. **HABITAT** Lakes. **DISTRIBUTION** North-Central and Eastern Provinces. **STATUS** SR.

Breeding

Oriental Darter
■ *Anhinga melanogaster*

DESCRIPTION Also known as Snakebird because of its snake-like appearance when submerged with just its long head and bill sticking out of the water. Looks superficially similar to the cormorants. **HABITAT** Lowland lakes. **DISTRIBUTION** Mainly dry zone. Occurs infrequently in wet lowlands. Found in same habitats as occupied by the Indian Cormorant, but no obvious reason why it is relatively scarce. **STATUS** UR; a relatively scarce bird.

Indian Thick-knee (Stone-curlew) ■ *Burhinus indicus*

DESCRIPTION Relatively large eyes. Can be distinguished from Great Thick-knee (see opposite) by strongly streaked body, and short, stubby, straight bill. Great Thick-knee has slightly upcurved bill. **HABITAT** Grassland in lowlands, often where there is adjoining scrub forest. **DISTRIBUTION** Mainly dry zone. Frequently overlooked in wet zone due to nocturnal habits. Often heard from golf course in central Colombo. **VOICE** Series of ascending *yip yip* notes when calling; these notes suddenly change in pitch. **STATUS** SR. Appears to be more scarce than Great Thick-knee.

Great Thick-knee ■ *Esacus recurvirostris*

DESCRIPTION Large eyes; mainly nocturnal. Not clear if it eats meat off carcasses or just pulls out invertebrates feeding on the carcass. Confusion possible with Indian Thick-knee (see opposite), but this species has more uniform upperparts and a long, upcurved bill. **HABITAT** Mainly dry lowlands in grassland. **DISTRIBUTION** Appears to be confined to dry lowlands close to coast. Feeds on invertebrates on grassland. It is unclear why it prefers grassland habitats with adjoining scrub forest close to coast. National parks such as Yala and Bundala are good sites in which to see it. **VOICE** Utters a melancholy *till-leowp*. Often heard at night – a signature of the dry-zone forests' nightscape. **STATUS** UR.

Eurasian Oystercatcher ■ *Haematopus ostralegus longipes*

DESCRIPTION Distinctive large, black-and-white wader with long red bill and long red legs. Black head, breast and upperparts, and white underparts. In flight shows broad white wing-bar. Juveniles have duller upperparts than adults. **HABITAT** Lowland marshes and wet habitats. **DISTRIBUTION** Can turn up anywhere on coast, on beaches and estuaries. Known localities include Bundala, Chilaw Sand Spit and Mannar Causeway. **VOICE** High-pitched, loud *tleep* note repeated quickly when excited. Also repeated more slowly when making contact. **STATUS** SM.

Black-winged Stilt ■ *Himantopus himantopus himantopus*

DESCRIPTION Females have browner backs than males. Juveniles marked with grey on face and hindneck. **HABITAT** Fresh and brackish waterbodies in lowlands.

Male

DISTRIBUTION During the migrant season there is an influx of birds to the wet zone, but they are almost entirely absent from this zone at other times. It is highly likely that birds resident in the dry zone are joined by migrants from the Asian mainland. Most birds in the wet zone are these birds. In April 2010, however, the second record occurred of these birds breeding in the wet zone in Talangama. Possibly half a dozen pairs had attempted to nest and at least two pairs raised young. In winter some birds are seen with a black hindneck, reminiscent of Australian Stilt, which is another subspecies. It is likely that these birds are also migrants from the Asian mainland. **VOICE** Shrill, insistent *ack ack*. **STATUS** CR, M.

Pacific Golden Plover ■ *Pluvialis fulva*

DESCRIPTION Buff to golden tips on mantle feathers; these tips occupy about half the visible length and are heart shaped on close examination. In non-breeding plumage Pacific Golden and Grey Plovers (see opposite) are superficially similar, but Grey is greyer and always has diagnostic black axillaries. In breeding plumage bases of wing feathers turn black, contrasting strongly with their golden tips, hence the name 'golden plover'.

Advanced ID notes Distinguished from **European Golden Plover** *Pluvialis apricaria* by white rather than grey-brown axillaries and inner-wing lining. Toes project beyond tail in Pacific, but not in European. **American Golden Plover** *Pluvialis dominica*, not likely to be seen in Sri Lanka, has brown axillaries and wing lining. Vagrant to Europe, where this feature is useful in distinguishing it from European. **HABITAT** Wet pastures and short-cropped grassland in lowlands. Habitat preference different from that of Grey. **DISTRIBUTION** Throughout lowlands on coast or close to it. Does occupy wet meadows, usually within a few kilometres of coast. **VOICE** Repeated high, fluty notes, *tee too whee-oh*. **STATUS** M. Occurs in small flocks.

Grey Plover ■ *Pluvialis squatarola*

DESCRIPTION Black axillaries (armpits) diagnostic in all plumages. In winter dark mantle feathers have pale, almost white edges. Lacks buff to golden tips on mantle feathers of golden plovers. **HABITAT** In small numbers in mudflats on estuaries, lagoons and salt pans. **DISTRIBUTION** Throughout coastal strip, mainly in dry lowlands. **VOICE** Double-noted, high-pitched *pee wee* call. **STATUS** UM.

LEFT: *Winter*, RIGHT: *Summer*

Little Ringed Plover ■ *Charadrius dubius curonicus*

DESCRIPTION Yellow eye-ring and very thin white wing-bar distinguish this species from **Common Ringed Plover** *Charadrius hiaticula tundrae*. Juveniles generally similar, but Little may show traces of a yellow orbital ring and its tertials extend over the primary tips. In breeding plumage eye-ring bright and swollen. Prominent black breast-band across white underparts, black oval patch below eye and black band on crown behind white forehead. **HABITAT** Open areas, especially mudflats in dry lowlands. At times on ploughed paddy fields. **DISTRIBUTION** Migrant birds appear in wet zone. **VOICE** Repeated, high-pitched, tremulous *phew* note. **STATUS** *C. d. curonicus* UM; *C. d. jerdoni* UR.

Acquiring breeding plumage

Kentish Plover ■ *Charadrius alexandrinus*

DESCRIPTION Smallest of plovers seen in Sri Lanka. White underparts and sandy-brown upperparts. In breeding plumage develops small black wedge adjoining corner of wing. In non-breeding plumage this becomes brown and indistinct. Can be distinguished

from Lesser Sand Plover (see below) by smaller size and slimmer bill, which is more pointed. Head also flatter on crown. Develops rust-brown on crown in breeding plumage. **HABITAT** Mudflats, sandbanks and short-cropped grassland in coastal areas. **DISTRIBUTION** All around coastal regions, but absent where coastline is developed. **VOICE** Whistled note; short *chwitz*, sounding more like that of a passerine. **STATUS** C. a. alexandrinus UR; C. a. seebohmi UM.

Breeding

Lesser Sand Plover ■ *Charadrius mongolus atrifrons*

DESCRIPTION During most of its stay in Sri Lanka this is a nondescript sandy-brown

plover with white underparts. Often congregates in large flocks. Shorter and small billed compared with Greater Sand Plover (see opposite). Develops black mask and orange-buff breast-band in breeding plumage. **HABITAT** Open, short-cropped grassland in dry lowlands. Most abundant near coast, where it also frequents tidal habitats. In wet zone can turn up on wet meadows. A flock regularly occupies Kotte Marshes near Colombo. **DISTRIBUTION** Throughout lowlands, but mainly in dry lowlands. **VOICE** High-pitched piping notes interspersed with tremulous notes. **STATUS** M.

Winter

Greater Sand Plover ■ *Charadrius leschenaultii leschenaultii*

DESCRIPTION Black mask and orange-buff breast-band in breeding plumage. Heavier billed and with longer-legged appearance than Lesser Sand Plover (see opposite). Legs pale green. This species appears a bit top heavy as it is longer legged than Lesser, and appears to be supporting a greater body mass. It takes time and practice to tell the two species apart. Greater prefers coastal habitats that are estuarine, and is usually seen in ones and twos. This also provides a clue to its identity. **HABITAT** Estuarine mudflats in dry lowlands. Also seen on beaches, but for feeding moves into areas swept by tide. **DISTRIBUTION** Disperses around coastline after arrival. Northern half of Sri Lanka may be the best place to see it as it has large areas of coastal estuaries. **VOICE** Rapid, tremulous, high-pitched notes. **STATUS** SM. Compared with Lesser, appears in relatively small numbers.

Winter

Caspian Plover

■ *Charadrius asiaticus*

DESCRIPTION In non-breeding plumage similar to **Oriental Plover** *Charadrius veredus*. Legs grey-green and white wing-bar more distinct than faint wing-bar in Oriental. May be seen with flocks of Lesser Sand Plover (see opposite), from which it can be distinguished by its longer legs, sharp, pointed bill and thick white supercilium extending behind eye. **HABITAT** Mudflats and lagoon edges in dry lowlands. **DISTRIBUTION** May turn up anywhere in coastal habitats. **STATUS** SM. A few records at the most each year.

Yellow-wattled Lapwing ■ *Vanellus malabaricus*

DESCRIPTION Sexes similar, with both having pronounced yellow lappets on face. Dark cap bordered in white below. Breast brown and not black as in Red-wattled Lapwing (see below). **HABITAT** Open areas in dry lowlands. Prefers dry, short-cropped grassland. Does not occur on damp meadows as does Red-wattled. Feeds on invertebrates, worms, insects and so on; hunts by picking or pulling prey from the ground and surface vegetation. **DISTRIBUTION** Dry lowlands, especially in arid-zone areas. **VOICE** Main call a drawn-out, screechy single note that is repeated. **STATUS** UR.

Red-wattled Lapwing
■ *Vanellus indicus lankae*

DESCRIPTION Brown upperparts; underparts and sides of face and neck white. White contrasts strongly with black cap, nape and black breast. Legs yellow as in Yellow-wattled Lapwing (see above). Overall impression is of black-and-white plover with red on lores and base of bill. **HABITAT** Wet habitats. May occupy small wetland patches even in cities. **DISTRIBUTION** Common throughout Sri Lanka. **VOICE** Call likened to 'did he do it', which is an onomatopoeic common name for the species. **STATUS** CR.

Greater Painted-snipe ■ *Rostratula benghalensis benghalensis*

DESCRIPTION Female more brightly coloured than male; another example of reversal of the usual sexual dimorphism. Prominent white band on body; band curves over wings in an arc. Eye encircled by white ring with line extending to back, like a white horizontal 'comma' sign. Bill shorter and slightly downcurved unlike snipes' straight bills. Male has yellowish barring on wing and is more patterned than female. **HABITAT** Marshes and paddy fields in lowlands. Often overlooked due to its discreet habits. Nocturnal. **DISTRIBUTION** Throughout lowlands. **VOICE** Single-note *wonk*, repeated. Very amphibian-like in quality and often overlooked for call of a frog. **STATUS** UR.

Male

Female

Pheasant-tailed Jacana ■ *Hydrophasianus chirurgus*

DESCRIPTION Non-breeding adults similar to juveniles, but show trace of yellow on neck. Breeding birds have showy long tails. Sexes look similar, but female is slightly bigger than male and has longer toes; a reversal of the usual size dimorphism of the sexes. **HABITAT** Lowland marshes and water-lily covered lakes. **DISTRIBUTION** Most common in dry zone. **VOICE** Liquid, bubbly *toonk toonk* calls. Also various mewing and screechy, grating calls. **STATUS** R.

Breeding

Whimbrel ■ *Numenius phaeopus*

DESCRIPTION Can be distinguished from similar Eurasian Curlew (see below) by its smaller size and shorter bill. Curlew's bill noticeably longer, and Whimbrel has median

stripe on crown. **HABITAT** Coastal mudflats, mangroves and brackish water habitats. Sometimes feeds on beaches in areas washed by waves. Curlew seldom seen on beaches. **DISTRIBUTION** May show up anywhere on coastlines, especially on beaches. Most common in dry lowlands; this may be a result of habitat destruction on wet-zone coastline. **VOICE** Rapidly repeated piping notes. **STATUS** UM. Two races, *N. p. phaeopus* and *N. p. variegatus*, have been recorded.

Eurasian Curlew ■ *Numenius arquata orientalis*

DESCRIPTION Can only be confused with smaller-sized and shorter-billed Whimbrel (see above). Elegant wader that stands tall among other waders. **HABITAT** Mudflats and

meadows beside coast. Appears to prefer freshwater meadows and damp grassland, where it can probe the ground for worms and other invertebrates. Does not like brackish habitats that Whimbrel favours. Even when seen inland on damp grassland, it is always within a few kilometres of the sea. **DISTRIBUTION** Coastal areas. **VOICE** Liquid, bubbling calls rising in intonation. Last note likened to 'curlew', hence the onomatopoeic common name. **STATUS** UM.

Black-tailed Godwit ■ *Limosa limosa*

DESCRIPTION White wing-bar and black tail-tip diagnostic, and easily distinguish this species from similar Bar-tailed Godwit (see below). Occurs in large flocks. In non-breeding plumage superficially similar to Bar-tailed, but longer legs, more uniformly grey upperparts and straight bill help to distinguish it from that species. In breeding plumage body turns rufous. Mantle and flight feathers have black centres notched with rufous. **HABITAT** Mudflats, estuaries and lagoons in lowlands. Occasionally marshes and paddy fields on passage. Most common in dry lowlands. **DISTRIBUTION** Throughout lowlands in coastal habitats. May be encountered in inland wetlands, usually no more than a few kilometres from the sea. **VOICE** Fast, repeated *wee-oh* that is thin and sounds urgent. **STATUS** M. Race *L. l. melanuroides*, known as **Eastern Black-tailed Godwit**, HSM.

Winter

Bar-tailed Godwit ■ *Limosa lapponica lapponica*

DESCRIPTION Shorter legged and streakier in appearance than Black-tailed Godwit (see above). Upturn in bill subtle but noticeable in the field. Mantle and flight feathers have dark shaft lines, giving birds a streaky appearance. In breeding plumage more rufous on underparts than in Black-tailed. **HABITAT** Similar to that of Black-tailed. Usually seen singly. **DISTRIBUTION** Coastal wetlands. Most records from area from Mannar to the Northern Peninsula. **VOICE** High-pitched *keek keek* calls, reminiscent of calls of Black-winged Stilt (see p. 58). Song a rapidly repeated single note. **STATUS** SM.

Winter

Ruddy Turnstone ▪ *Arenaria interpres interpres*

DESCRIPTION Plump and long body, low profile and broad-based bill make this wader easy to pick out. Body shape alone sufficient to tell turnstones apart from other waders. In non-breeding plumage upperparts dark with dark breast-band and dirty-white head. In summer mantle turns chestnut, and throat, breast and eye-patch turn jet-black. White band between mantle and neck breaks up black on neck. This seems to work as disruptive colouration, since if the birds are motionless they can be hard to pick out by predators. **HABITAT** Coastal mudflats, estuaries and similar. **DISTRIBUTION** On arrival migrants spread around coastal areas. Never far from the sea. **VOICE** Tremulous, bubbly call that is short in duration. **STATUS** M.

RIGHT: *Acquiring summer plumage*

Sanderling ▪ *Calidris alba*

DESCRIPTION Short black legs and short black bill. In winter looks all white with black patch on bend of wing. In winter plumage black shoulder-patch is concealed at times.

Winter

White wing-bar contrasts strongly with black trailing edge of wing and dark greater coverts, forming dark edge to front of white wing-bar. Juveniles have darker mantle than adults. In breeding plumage head, neck, mantle, scapulars and tertials acquire pale rufous tinge. Mantle feathers have thick black tips. Birds have a habit of running up and down as waves break on a shore. Usually seen in flocks of around 7–15 individuals. **HABITAT** Bird of coastline, where undisturbed and relatively unpolluted stretches can be found. **DISTRIBUTION** May turn up anywhere on sandy beaches; Chilaw Sand Spit is a reliable site. **VOICE** Sharp, slight, tremulous *zit* call. **STATUS** UM.

Little Stint ■ *Calidris minuta*

DESCRIPTION One of the smallest of the waders. Bill black and blunt tipped. White underparts. In winter plumage (which birds are in during most of their time in Sri Lanka), upperparts greyish, with mantle feathers having black shafts. In breeding plumage black shaft streaks widen into black centres with rusty-red edges. The tertials become black-centred with rusty-red edges. **HABITAT** Estuaries and mudflats in lowlands. Most common in dry lowlands. **DISTRIBUTION** Coastal areas, especially in dry zone. **VOICE** High-pitched, rapidly repeated and rising *tseep tseep tseep*. **STATUS** CM.

Summer

Curlew Sandpiper ■ *Calidris ferruginea*

DESCRIPTION Distinctive small wader with downcurved, long beak. In winter plumage (which birds are in during most of their time in Sri Lanka), shows white underparts with grey upperparts. Mantle and flight feathers grey with thin black shaft streaks. In breeding plumage, which some birds acquire before they leave Sri Lanka, head, neck and breast turn rufous. Mantle feathers have rusty bases with black 'trident' marking. This species has grey line bifurcating white rump. Vagrant **Dunlin** *Calidris alpina* has unbroken white rump. Species look very similar in winter and both have thin white wing-bars. In summer plumage Dunlin acquires black belly and lacks rufous found in Curlew Sandpiper. **HABITAT** Estuaries and mudflats in dry lowlands. **DISTRIBUTION** Throughout Sri Lanka on estuaries, salt pans and other coastal habitats. Bundala and the Palatupana Salt Pans are reliable sites for seeing flocks at close range. **VOICE** Rapid, tremulous, twittering call. The background call heard most frequently in estuaries in Sri Lanka where mixed wader flocks are found. **STATUS** CM.

Winter

Ruff ■ *Calidris pugnax*

DESCRIPTION Plump-bodied, small-headed appearance gives this wader a profile that helps to pick it out from a flock. Bigger than most of the *Calidris* waders, it is usually in mixed species concentrations. Mantle and wing feathers have pale edges, giving scalloped effect. Adult females and juveniles have all-dark bills. Adult female usually has brighter coloured yellowish legs than juveniles. Males show pale bills and are larger than females. **HABITAT** Mudflats, estuaries and lagoons in lowlands. **DISTRIBUTION** All around lowland coasts where suitable habitat is found. Salt pans are good places to look for it. **STATUS** UM.

Winter

Winter

Pintail Snipe ■ *Gallinago stenura*

DESCRIPTION The most common of the snipes – almost all of the snipes seen in Sri Lanka are Pintail Snipes. **Common Snipe** *Gallinago gallinago* is a scarce migrant to Sri Lanka and is best distinguished from Pintail by white trailing edges to secondaries in

flight. Even in the field, Common is noticeably longer billed to an observer familiar with Pintail. In Pintail buff stripe over eye is wider than black eye-line, where the two join base of bill, although this is not easily seen in the field. Underwing in Common paler at wing-base. **HABITAT** Paddy fields and marshes in lowlands. **DISTRIBUTION** Spreads throughout Sri Lanka in marshy habitats, all the way to highlands. **VOICE** When flushed, takes off with a harsh *kreik* call. Not guttural like voices of herons. **STATUS** M.

Common Redshank ■ *Tringa totanus*

DESCRIPTION Red legs and white wing-bar on upper wing make it easy to identify this wader. **Spotted Redshank** *Tringa erythropus*, a very scarce migrant, is similar looking. In flight absence of white wing-bar in Spotted makes identification easy. At rest Spotted and Common are similar, but Spotted has red on base of beak confined to lower mandible. However, note that juvenile Commons sometimes have reddish base confined to lower mandible, so wing-bar is best diagnostic feature. In breeding plumage Spotted very different from Common, with black head, neck and underparts; wings and mantle feathers turn black with pale edges. **HABITAT** Estuaries, lagoons and other brackish habitats. On passage in freshwater habitats like marshes and paddy fields. Most common in dry lowlands. **DISTRIBUTION** Mainly coastal areas, where it occupies mix of wetland habitats from freshwater marshes to mudflats and mangroves. Wintering birds tend to stop over only for brief periods in freshwater habitats in wet zone. In dry zone they occupy flooded fields and marshes not far from coast. **VOICE** Liquid, melodious *peeuw* of medium length distinctive; for many birders a key signature of a wader habitat. Birds very vocal; in Britain once known locally as 'wardens of the marshes', as they are quick to alert others of intruders. **STATUS** CM. Two subspecies recorded: *T. t. eurhinus* and *T. t. terrignotae*.

Summer

Common Greenshank ■ *Tringa nebularia*

DESCRIPTION Bill heavier and slightly more upturned than Marsh Sandpiper's (see p. 70). Heavier build. Bill often best field characteristic. See also notes under Marsh. Flight call also diagnostic. Juveniles have browner upperparts than adults, with pale edges. Adult winter birds grey with mantle feathers fringed with dark and pale double band. Tertials show traces of notched edges that become conspicuous in breeding plumage. Head and neck become streaked in summer plumage. **HABITAT** Paddy fields, estuaries, lagoons and similar in lowlands. **DISTRIBUTION** Prefers brackish wetlands. Also uses freshwater wetlands. Stops over in paddy fields and marshes on migration to southern dry-zone coastal wetlands. **VOICE** Single *kip kip* notes uttered in rapid sequence. In flight a double-noted *chew-chew*. Calls a little melodious. **STATUS** UM.

Summer

Marsh Sandpiper ■ *Tringa stagnatilis*

DESCRIPTION Pencil-thin bill, slender build and pale overall colour help identify this wader. Juveniles have dark mantles and flight feathers. In winter plumage adults plain with white heads and necks. Wing feathers pale edged. In breeding plumage head and neck flecked to form streaks. Wing and mantle feathers become light brown, and middle of mantle feathers has black markings. The black markings are reminiscent of raptor sillhouettes; this is only evident at very close range. In flight birds show long, narrow white wedge on upperparts (wide in Common Greenshank, see p. 69). Toes project well beyond tail. **HABITAT** Marshes, paddy fields, estuaries, lagoons and similar in lowlands. **DISTRIBUTION** Spreads around coastal habitats. One of the taller waders, often wading deep into pools. Sometimes spends a few days in freshwater marshes and paddy fields as it travels to and from its preferred coastal wetlands in dry lowlands. **VOICE** High-pitched, strident *pip pip*. **STATUS** CM.

Summer *Winter*

Green Sandpiper ■ *Tringa ochropus*

DESCRIPTION White supercilium does not extend behind eye – see also Wood Sandpiper (see opposite). In flight dark underwings give it a black-and-white appearance at a distance. **HABITAT** Prefers freshwater pools in lowlands. **DISTRIBUTION** Throughout lowlands, but seems to prefer dry lowlands. Occasionally seen in streams and other wet habitats in highlands. **VOICE** Can make a series of rapid *pip pip* notes followed by longer fluty notes. Flight call 2–3 *thchew thchew* notes, which are clean and clear. **STATUS** UM.

Winter

Wood Sandpiper ■ *Tringa glareola*

DESCRIPTION Pale underwings – Green Sandpiper (see opposite) has dark underwings. Pale supercilium extending beyond eye also distinguishes this species from Green. Heavy speckling on upperparts separates it from Green and Common Sandpipers (see pp. 70 and 72). Greenish-yellow legs, taller than in Common. **HABITAT** Marshes, paddy fields, estuaries, lagoons and similar in lowlands. **DISTRIBUTION** Spreads all over lowlands in marshy habitats. A few make their way up to hills, but this is not typical. Most seen in wet zone seem to stop over on passage to wetlands in southern half of Sri Lanka. **VOICE** Flight call reminiscent of Common's, but less thin and more liquid-like in quality. Other calls include piping notes repeated frequently. **STATUS** M.

Winter

Terek Sandpiper ■ *Xenus cinereus*

DESCRIPTION Short-legged wader with long, upturned beak and distinctive profile. Legs yellowish (but note that leg colour may be masked by mud). Bill has diffused yellow patch at base. Greyish-brown upperparts with faint edges to feathers. Looks uniformly coloured in the field. Juveniles have thick edges to wing feathers. **HABITAT** Coastal mudflats, salt pans and estuaries in dry lowlands. **DISTRIBUTION** Confined to mudflats and mangroves on coast. May turn up anywhere there is suitable habitat. Numbers highest in coastal wetlands in northern half of Sri Lanka. **VOICE** Melancholy whistled or piped notes of medium length; sometimes preceded by rapid double note. **STATUS** UM.

Winter

Common Sandpiper ▪ *Actitis hypoleucos*

DESCRIPTION 'White finger' curving around bend of wing a useful field characteristic.

Stiff winged in flight, and shows clear white wing-bar. Habit of bobbing tail. **HABITAT** Marshes, paddy fields, estuaries, lagoons and similar, mainly in lowlands. Sometimes along streams and canals. **DISTRIBUTION** Anywhere in Sri Lanka. In highlands usually seen near watercourses. **VOICE** High-pitched *tsee tsee tsee* notes, usually uttered in flight. **STATUS** M.

Winter

Barred Buttonquail (Barred Bustard-quaile)

▪ *Turnix suscitator leggei*

DESCRIPTION Role of sexes is reversed in this species, and this is reflected in the plumage. Female has black chin and throat, and black-and-white barring on upper breast and sides of neck; brighter than male. Males incubate eggs and look after young. Female lays clutch of eggs and may move on to find another male to mate with and lay another clutch of eggs. **HABITAT** Scrub jungle. **DISTRIBUTION** Mainly seen in dry-zone scrub jungles; occasionally in wet zone. **VOICE** Similar to throb of motorbike or low-frequency engine. **STATUS** R.

LEFT: *Male*, RIGHT: *Female*

Crab-plover ▪ *Dromas ardeola*

DESCRIPTION Black-and-white, stoutly built wader with conical, thick black bill. **Pied Avocets** *Recurvirostra avosetta*, also black-and-white waders, have thin, upturned bills and are longer necked with black crowns. Juvenile Crab-plovers duller than adults, with greyish or dirty-white mantles. In flight black flight feathers contrast with white forewing. Disruptive colouration against a dull greyish-brown mudflat can at times make it surprisingly hard to pick out these birds. **HABITAT** Mudflats in estuaries, tidal lagoons and similar, where it can hunt for marine and other tide-line invertebrates, including crabs. **DISTRIBUTION** Scarce breeding resident in north-west Sri Lanka, in strip to north from Mannar. Birds may take part in local migrations and have been seen on south-east coasts. It cannot be ruled out that some birds may be migrants from mainland Asia. **VOICE** Three-noted call that sounds like *ka-hee-kew*; distinct call that cuts through background noise. Some calls reminiscent of a puppy yelping. **STATUS** SR.

Indian Courser ▪ *Cursorius coromandelicus*

DESCRIPTION Coursers are like plovers with shortish, downcurved, pointed bills. This is the only courser found in Sri Lanka. Adults have chestnut crowns and necks. Face has black line from base of bill to nape, with white line over it. Juveniles have the stripes, but in shades of brown and white; mantle feathers edged with white. **HABITAT** Dry lowland grassland close to coast. Appears to frequent grass taller than that used by birds such as lapwings. When feeding runs in little spurts in plover-like fashion. **DISTRIBUTION** Recently only known from a few sites in the Mannar district, although there are older records from the Jaffna Peninsula. Occurs in small flocks of around half a dozen individuals in known sites. One of Sri Lanka's rarest resident birds. **STATUS** HSR. Classified as Critically Endangered on IUCN Red List.

Breeding

Small Pratincole
■ *Glareola lactea*

DESCRIPTION Easily told apart in flight from similar **Oriental** and **Collared Pratincoles** *Glareola maldivarum* and *G. pratincola* by conspicuous black-and-white wing-bars on flight feathers. Inner primaries show some white on trailing edges. In breeding plumage has black line from bill to eye. Tail only weakly forked. Black underwing-coverts that show in flight. **HABITAT** Open areas adjoining waterbodies in dry lowlands. **DISTRIBUTION** Dry lowlands close to coast. Often seen in small flocks. **VOICE** Metallic grating note repeated regularly. **STATUS** UR. Classified as Vulnerable on IUCN Red List.

Brown Noddy ■ *Anous stolidus pileatus*

DESCRIPTION Pale bar across upper-wing coverts contrasts with flight feathers. Underwing-coverts paler and contrast with dark flight feathers, but not apparent unless

lighting conditions permit. Chocolate-brown tail contrasts with paler back. Pale forehead extends to crown; can be very white in some birds. Lores dark, looking black. Bill more downcurved than Lesser Noddy's (see opposite). Bill heavy and jagged compared with Lesser's. Wing flaps in flight distinctly slower and more laboured than those of Lesser. Tail bigger and more spoon shaped than Lesser's. Brown also has a habit of bringing its tail down at right angles to the body when it needs to brake air speed. **HABITAT** Pelagic. **DISTRIBUTION** Pelagic, passage visitor just before south-west monsoon strikes Sri Lanka. Seas off Kalpitiya seem to be best location; also seen occasionally by whale watchers from boats off Mirissa. **VOICE** Repeated grunting note. **STATUS** UM.

Lesser Noddy ■ *Anous tenuirostris tenuirostris*

DESCRIPTION Smaller than Brown Noddy (see opposite) with fine, long bill. Greyish lores contrast with dark around eye. Lores often look white and in some birds this extends to crown, nape and upper back. More white on forehead than shown in illustrations in many field guides. Underwing uniformly brown, lacking contrast of Brown's. Wingbeats quicker than Brown's. **HABITAT** Pelagic. **DISTRIBUTION** Pelagic, passage visitor just before south-west monsoon strikes Sri Lanka. Seas off Kalpitiya seem to be best location; also seen occasionally by whale watchers from boats off Mirissa. **STATUS** HSM. Probably under-recorded like many other pelagics.

Lesser Black-backed Gull ■ (ssp. Heuglin's Gull) (*Larus fuscus*)

DESCRIPTION Breeding adult has dark grey upperparts with distinctive white trailing edges to wings. **Yellow-legged Gull** *Larus michahellis* has paler upperparts and different pattern on wing-tips. Juveniles have dark tail-tips and dark brown flight feathers. The taxonomy of white-headed gulls remains in flux and the **Steppe Gull** *Larus [heuglini] barabensis* is currently treated by some as a subspecies of Heuglin's Gull. Steppe has paler back and white spot on outer two primaries. Juveniles whiter on head and underparts than juvenile Heuglin's. Steppe is a vagrant to Sri Lanka and may be overlooked. **HABITAT** Mainly coastal areas. **DISTRIBUTION** Northern parts of Sri Lanka. **VOICE** Nasal, drawn-out call notes. Very similar to those of **Lesser Black-backed Gull** *L. f. graellsii* race, common in Europe. **STATUS** M.

LEFT: *Immature*, RIGHT: *Adult*

Great Black-headed (Pallas's) Gull ■ *Larus ichthyaetus*

DESCRIPTION Large size and tricoloured bill. Juveniles have grey on mantle. Lacks 'white mirrors' on dark primary tips found on Brown-headed Gull (see below). Dark irises.

HABITAT Seagoing bird. During the day often roosts on open fields. **DISTRIBUTION** Most common in the Northern Peninsula. Kora Kulam in Mannar is a reliable site for roosting gulls. **VOICE** Deep murmuring call with a melancholy accent. **STATUS** M.

Acquiring summer plumage

Brown-headed Gull ■ *Larus brunnicephalus*

DESCRIPTION Similar to Common Black-headed Gull. Brown-headed has 'wing-tips dipped in black ink', with white mirror between point of wing-tip and concave base of black triangle. Pale iris (dark in Great Black-headed, see above) and slightly more distinct pale eye-ring than in Great Black-headed give it a different look. In breeding plumage head turns chocolate-brown. In winter white head has smudgy 'headphones' pattern. First winter has black terminal band on tail and banding on wing-coverts. **HABITAT** Coastal locations in relatively unpolluted or undisturbed areas. **DISTRIBUTION** Around coastline; concentrated in areas where fish are brought ashore. Numbers highest in northern half of Sri Lanka. **VOICE** Strident mewing call. **STATUS** M.

LEFT: *Summer*, RIGHT: *Winter*

Gull-billed Tern ▪ *Gelochelidon nilotica nilotica*

DESCRIPTION Heavy dark bill. Breeding adult has black cap. In non-breeding plumage eye has dark smudge extending behind it. Crown shows traces of black cap. **HABITAT** Widespread visitor to lowland waterbodies. Most common along coastal areas. On arrival spreads widely in coastal areas. **DISTRIBUTION** Mainly found on coastline patrolling beaches. **VOICE** Double-noted *cheez-weet*, alternating in pitch. Nasal, and cuts through the air. **STATUS** SR, CM.

Summer

Caspian Tern ▪ *Hydroprogne caspia*

DESCRIPTION Large tern with sturdy red bill and legs. Black crown in summer; in winter forehead white with traces of black. Leading primaries black or dusky on underwing, and upper wing tipped black. Black legs. Unlikely to be confused with other terns in Sri Lanka. Juvenile has scaly mantle with greyish feathers edged in brown. Black crown is underdeveloped. **HABITAT** Coast, salt pans and estuaries. May occasionally be seen hunting over freshwater bodies not far from coast. **DISTRIBUTION** Mainly coastal areas. Congregates in sites such as salt pans. **VOICE** Drawn-out, screechy whistle. Also some harsh, grating calls. **STATUS** SR, M.

Lesser Crested Tern ■ *Thalasseus bengalensis bengalensis*

DESCRIPTION Orangish bill separates this species from larger Great Crested Tern (see below), which has yellow bill. **HABITAT** Seagoing tern that can be seen roosting in brackish-water habitats (salt pans, estuaries and similar). **DISTRIBUTION** All around coastal areas. **VOICE** Grating, tremulous *thureep* and variations on this theme. **STATUS** M

Winter

Great (Large) Crested Tern ■ *Thalasseus bergii*

DESCRIPTION Greenish-yellow bill. Shallow and measured wingbeats – viewed directly from below birds look as though they are hardly beating their wings at all. Engages in plunge diving to catch fish. **HABITAT** Seagoing tern that can be seen roosting in brackish water habitats (salt pans, estuaries and similar). **DISTRIBUTION** All around coastal areas. **VOICE** Harsh, far-carrying *kraa*. **STATUS** Race *T. b. velox* R; race *T. b. thalassina* V.

Non-breeding

Common Tern ■ *Sterna hirundo*

DESCRIPTION Juveniles and winter birds show dark carpal bar in flight and at rest. Bill longer than in *Childonias* marsh terns. In the hand or on close views, bill looks stouter. In summer bill and legs are red. In winter legs can turn black; in some birds they retain varying degrees of redness. Outer primaries dull black. Mantle and upperparts grey. Black cap recedes exposing white forehead. Birds seen are believed to belong to race *S. h. longipennis*. It is possible that race *S. h. tibetana* also occurs here. **HABITAT** Coastal areas; roosts in salt pans, estuaries and similar. **DISTRIBUTION** Widespread on arrival in coastal areas. Overlooked in the past because many observers were unable to identify the species. The author has found it to be a regular visitor to the strip from Chilaw Sand Spit to Mannar. **VOICE** Loud, grating *kraa* calls alternating with high-pitched, shrieking *kree* notes. **STATUS** Most birds M; also believed to be SR.

Winter

Little Tern ■ *Sternula albifrons sinensis*

DESCRIPTION Smallest of the terns, with pointed wings and rapid, butterfly-like, fluttering flight. In breeding plumage develops black crown with white forehead, and black line from base of bill through eye to back of black crown. Yellow bill with black tip. In non-breeding birds bill all black, but may retain yellow base. Black crown recedes further from white forehead and is more diffused and duller. Scarce **Saunders's Tern** *Sternula saundersi* has a squarer white forehead without a hint of the white supercilium seen in breeding plumage of Little. **HABITAT** Frequents both coast and inland freshwater lakes in lowlands. **DISTRIBUTION** Breeding resident in dry zone and visitor to wet zone. Breeding birds may be supplemented by wintering birds from Asian mainland, but this is to be proven. **VOICE** Repeated, high-pitched *chick chick*. **STATUS** R.

Winter

Bridled (Brown-winged) Tern ▪ *Onychoprion anaethetus*

DESCRIPTION Uniform grey-brown upperparts in adults, and pale under-body. Tail brownish. Can look black in adverse lighting. In adult upper tail and upper-tail coverts are

brown. Underwing-coverts white with flight feathers brown. Wing-coverts and mantle slightly paler brown than primaries, but this is not obvious in the field. White extends over eye forming short but thick supercilium. In juveniles upper-tail coverts can be pale. Bill looks long and thin compared with bills of other terns. Adult has elongated outer-tail feathers; the 'tail streamers'. **HABITAT** Pelagic. Large numbers pass along west coast in August–September. **DISTRIBUTION** One of the most frequently seen seabirds on whale watches, but seen only by a tiny handful of shore-based birdwatchers before May 2008. **STATUS** CM, HSR.

Whiskered Tern ▪ *Chlidonias hybrida hybrida*

DESCRIPTION In breeding plumage reddish bill and black crown contrast with white cheeks. Legs reddish. Belly turns black, contrasting with whitish underwing. Under-

tail white. In non-breeding plumage bill and legs black, forehead white; dark smudge over eye and traces of black crown on rear end of crown towards nape. Juveniles like non-breeding adults, with dark mantles scalloped with white edges to mantle feathers. **HABITAT** Freshwater lakes and marshes with open stretches of water. Occasionally seen on beaches, especially before return migration. **DISTRIBUTION** On arrival spreads up to mid-hills. **VOICE** Repeated, metallic *krick*. **STATUS** CM.

Summer

White-winged Tern ■ *Chlidonias leucopterus*

DESCRIPTION In all plumages this species has a contrasting white tail and rump. In breeding plumage black underwing easily separates it from Whiskered Tern (see opposite). Non-breeding birds may be confused with **Black Tern** *Chlidonias niger*, which occurs as a vagrant to south Asia. Black has more forked tail and grey rump (white in White-winged). Non-breeding Black has greyish-brown side-patches, and broader black patch on cheek linked to black patch on hind-crown. Breeding birds have smoky-black upperparts unlike strongly contrasting white wings on breeding White-winged. **HABITAT** Freshwater lakes, lagoons and similar in lowlands. **DISTRIBUTION** On arrival spreads around lowlands, not ascending as high as Whiskered. Seems to favour dry lowlands. **VOICE** *Krick* call, more highly pitched than that of Whiskered. **STATUS** M.

Ceylon Bay Owl
■ *Phodilus assimilis*

DESCRIPTION Barn-owl like, triangular facial disc with dark crown. Flight feathers barred and mantle feathers have lines of black-and-white dots. Upperparts darker with hint of chestnut. Stout build. **HABITAT** Known only from good-quality forests. **DISTRIBUTION** Wet zone up to highest mountains, and also intermediate zone. **VOICE** Three-syllable whistle that sounds a little like *oh-kee-yow*. Slightly tremulous. **STATUS** HSR. One of the least seen bird species. Not observed in the wild in Sri Lanka for years until 2001.

Brown Boobook (Brown Hawk-owl) ■ *Ninox scutulata hirsuta*

DESCRIPTION About the size of a crow with largely plain upperparts. Underparts white with lines of heavy rufous spots, leaving a few areas of white on breast. All white around vent. **HABITAT** Has adapted to urban environments, and in cities such as Colombo uses TV aerials as substitutes for tall perches. **DISTRIBUTION** Widespread throughout Sri Lanka. **VOICE** Distinctive *ku wook ku wook* call that is repeated. Sometimes utters same call softly, making it seem much further away than it really is. Rarely, utters yelping call. **STATUS** R.

Jungle Owlet
■ *Glaucidium radiatum radiatum*

DESCRIPTION Small owl barred with black and white. Face and underparts similar to Chestnut-backed Owlet's (see opposite), but confusion unlikely when upperparts are seen. Active by day. **HABITAT** Mainly lowland scrub jungles. **DISTRIBUTION** Dry zone. Seems to be abundant in Moneragala-Nilgala area. **VOICE** Some call notes similar to Chestnut-backed Owlet's. Utters series of almost barking-like *ooh ooh* notes that are slightly tremulous. Alternates with more insistent barking *oo oo* notes. **STATUS** R.

Chestnut-backed Owlet ■ *Glaucidium castanotum* ⓔ

DESCRIPTION Face and underparts similar to Jungle Owlet's (see opposite), but chestnut upperparts easily separate the two species. **HABITAT** Well-wooded areas, although it is not shy and may roost near human habitation where it adjoins good-quality forest. **DISTRIBUTION** Confined to wet zone. Probably more common than it is believed to be. Interestingly, Jungle and Chestnut-backed Owlets seem to carve out different areas in Sri Lanka. **VOICE** Higher pitched than Jungle's; more like a throaty tremulous *kruk kruk*. Also a repeated single-noted *wheeuw*, which it alternates in pitch from one note to another and repeats. **STATUS** E. Classified as Vulnerable on IUCN Red List.

Serendib Scops-owl ■ *Otus thilohoffmanni* ⓔ

DESCRIPTION Overall reddish hue and soft, single-note call help make confusion with other birds unlikely. Male has orangish irides; female's are yellowish. Each pair is believed to maintain a territory year-round. **HABITAT** Disturbed forest edges, often near the ground. Appears to be insectivorous. **DISTRIBUTION** Restricted to a few lowland rainforests such as Sinharaja, Morapitiya and Kithulgala. **VOICE** Call a soft *phew*. **STATUS** SE, first seen in 2001. Described to science only in 2004 by Deepal Warakagoda (who discovered it) and Pamela Rasmussen. First endemic bird to be described from Sri Lanka after 132 years – it is amazing that an endemic Sri Lankan bird eluded being known for so long. Its scientific name honours Thilo Hoffmann, who is credited with leading the campaign to halt the destruction of the Sinharaja Rainforest.

Indian Scops-owl ▪ *Otus bakkamoena bakkamoena*

DESCRIPTION Brown irides help to distinguish this species from rarer **Oriental Scops-owl** *Otus sunia*. Two colour forms, one greyish, the other rufous. Marked less on underparts

than Oriental, and some grey-form birds less marked than rufous forms. Ear-tufts well formed and often erected. **HABITAT** Village and town gardens, and secondary forest. Has adapted to urban habitats. **DISTRIBUTION** Throughout Sri Lanka from lowlands to highlands. The most common and widespread of the owls. **VOICE** Very vocal during breeding season. Utters a *whuk whuk* call. Sometimes a series of notes is rapidly uttered. **STATUS** R.

Spot-bellied Eagle-owl
▪ *Bubo nipalensis blighi*

DESCRIPTION Large owl with prominent 'horns' on head. Underparts have downwards-pointing arrowheads. Flight feathers barred and wing-coverts patterned in middle, lending an overall impression of barring and mottling. Juveniles paler than adults. **HABITAT** Frequents tracts of large forests, but most sightings by birders are where it has roosted close to human habitation adjoining forests. **DISTRIBUTION** Throughout Sri Lanka up to highlands. Most records from large tracts of lowland dry-zone and wet-zone jungles. **VOICE** Whistle that sounds like a nasal and slightly explosive *kee yow*. **STATUS** UR.

Brown Fish-owl
▪ *Ketupa zeylonensis zeylonensis*

DESCRIPTION Large size, prominent yellow eyes and distinct thin streaks on underparts. Upperparts heavily marked and wings barred. Partly diurnal and the owl most seen by visitors to national parks. **HABITAT** Widespread up to mid-hills. Tolerant of human habitation. **DISTRIBUTION** Widespread from lowlands to highlands. Grounds of the Cinnamon Lodge and Chaaya Village at Habarana are reliable sites. Often seen roosting on large Kumbuk trees adjoining freshwater lakes, for example at Habarana. **VOICE** Double-noted, deep *uhm-ooom*. **STATUS** R.

Black-winged Kite ▪ *Elanus caeruleus vociferus*

DESCRIPTION Small white raptor with black shoulders. Habit of hovering like a kestrel. **HABITAT** Open grassland. Sometimes seen perched on overhead wires. **DISTRIBUTION** Widespread; most common in dry zone and hills. It was never particularly abundant, but appears to have been declining over the years. Use of pesticides may have reduced its prey base. **VOICE** One call is a nasal *hweet*; does not sound typically raptor-like. **STATUS** UR.

Oriental Honey-buzzard ▪ *Pernis ptilorhynchus*

DESCRIPTION Identified by relatively small-sized head, giving it a pigeon-headed look. Dark and light phases occur. Colouration highly variable. **HABITAT** Found where pockets of jungle are interspersed with open areas. As the species' name suggests, it likes raiding honeycombs. **DISTRIBUTION** Throughout Sri Lanka. **VOICE** Short, high-pitched wail. **STATUS** UR, SM. Occurs as resident race, *ruficollis*, which is supplemented by migrant race *orientalis* during the northern winter.

Crested Serpent-eagle ▪ *Spilornis cheela spilogaster*

DESCRIPTION Yellow irides, yellow cere, brown body with white spotting, dark crown and distinct nuchal crest help separate this species from Crested Hawk-eagle (see

p. 92). Juvenile Crested Serpent-eagles that appear whitish can be distinguished from juvenile Crested Hawk-eagles by lack of feathering on legs. **HABITAT** Forests and scrub. Takes a wide variety of small animals. **DISTRIBUTION** Throughout Sri Lanka. **VOICE** Repeated, double-noted call, more strident and higher pitched than similar call of Crested Hawk-eagle. **STATUS** R.

Black Kite
▪ *Milvus migrans govinda*

DESCRIPTION Uniformly brown. Forked tail separates this species from juvenile Brahminy Kites (see below). **HABITAT** Open areas. Diet mainly small mammals, birds and invertebrates. Can also be seen scavenging at refuse dumps. **DISTRIBUTION** Mainly the Northern Peninsula along coast. Occasionally turns up in dry lowlands of south. **STATUS** SR, M.

Brahminy Kite ▪ *Haliastur indus indus*

DESCRIPTION Adults have white head and brick-coloured wings. Juveniles brown and may be confused with Black Kite (see above), but latter has forked tail. Juvenile Brahminy has dark underwing-coverts that contrast with underwing, and lacks dark tail-tip of juvenile Black. **HABITAT** Hunts over open water, paddy fields and open areas. Seems to prefer areas near water. Needs tall trees for nesting. Marked preference for fish but will take other small animals. **DISTRIBUTION** Lowlands and mid-hills. **VOICE** Generally a silent bird. When gathering to roost often utters nasal yelping call from overhead. **STATUS** R.

White-bellied Sea-eagle ■ *Haliaeetus leucogaster*

DESCRIPTION Largest of Sri Lanka's eagles. Adults have white bodies and grey wings. Juveniles brown. In flight holds wings at strong dihedral (upturned into a shallow V). **HABITAT** Near waterbodies, especially in coastal areas. Mostly bird of dry lowlands, although a few individuals occur in wet zone up to mid-hills. Feeds mainly on fish, but also takes small mammals. **DISTRIBUTION** Mainly dry lowlands, but can occur anywhere. **VOICE** Rapidly repeated, agitated notes that sound as though more than one bird is calling. **STATUS** UR.

Grey-headed Fish-eagle ■ *Ichthyophaga ichthyaetus*

DESCRIPTION Large eagle with grey head and brown wings. **HABITAT** Always found around open lakes with tall trees for roosting and nesting. **DISTRIBUTION** Dry lowlands. **VOICE** During breeding season pairs duet, engaging in a series of melancholy and haunting calls, some of which sound like a person being strangled. In Uda Walawe National Park they can be heard calling at night. **STATUS** SR; nationally endangered bird.

Pallid Harrier

■ *Circus macrourus*

DESCRIPTION Adult male Pallid Harrier easily distinguished from adult male Montagu's Harrier (see below) by black bar on bases of upper secondaries in latter. Upperparts grey in both males. Females and juveniles in shades of brown; identification quite complex. Pallid has tip of wing formed by primaries 2–4 and prominent pale collar, and penultimate band on under-tail appears as dark blob and has dark secondaries. More advanced texts should be consulted for juveniles and females. **HABITAT** Open grassland, where it hunts for rodents and birds. **DISTRIBUTION** Winter visitor throughout Sri Lanka to dry lowlands. **STATUS** UR.

Female

Montagu's Harrier

■ *Circus pygargus*

DESCRIPTION See Pallid Harrier (above) for notes on identification. Male is easily identified by grey upperwing and black bases to secondaries. Females of Montagu's and Pallid are similar and more advanced texts need to be consulted to distinguish them. **HABITAT** Hunts over open grassland. Feeds on small animals, especially rodents and birds found in open areas. **DISTRIBUTION** Migrant to open areas of dry zone. Most common in the Northern Peninsula. **STATUS** UM.

Male

Shikra ▪ *Accipiter badius badius*

DESCRIPTION Similar looking to **Besra Sparrowhawk** *Accipiter virgatus*, which has longitudinal streaking on throat extending to breast. Besra also has white on throat, sharply demarcated from grey on sides of face. Adult Shikra lacks upper-tail barring found in Besra. Occasionally takes to soaring. **HABITAT** Forests, and wooded parts of towns and cities. Needs pockets of dense cover. Preys on small animals including birds, reptiles, mammals and amphibians. **DISTRIBUTION** Throughout Sri Lanka. **VOICE** Occasionally takes to soaring and uttering loud, screaming call from the air. Call usually series of shrill, single *kiew, kiew, kiew* or double-noted *ki-kiew ki-kiew ki-kiew* notes. **STATUS** R.

Eurasian Buzzard ▪ *Buteo buteo vulpinus*

DESCRIPTION Medium-sized in relation to other Sri Lankan birds of prey. Brown overall.

Rounded head is best guide. May be confused with juvenile Brahminy Kite (see p. 87), but underwing pattern of juvenile Brahminy is different. Buzzards wintering in Sri Lanka have different morphs – advanced texts should be consulted on these. **HABITAT** Often found where forest cover borders grassland. Takes small animals such as birds, mammals and reptiles. **DISTRIBUTION** Migrant to highland areas such as Horton Plains National Park. **STATUS** SM.

Black Eagle ■ *Ictinaetus malayensis perniger*

DESCRIPTION Medium-sized dark eagle with yellow cere and feet. **HABITAT** Forests and high ridges with forest cover. Takes small animals such as birds, mammals and lizards. Giant squirrels seem to be a preferred prey item. **DISTRIBUTION** Throughout forested areas, but mainly in wet zone and especially in mid-hills and highlands. **STATUS** UR.

Rufous-bellied Eagle ■ *Lophotriorchis kienerii*

DESCRIPTION Adult distinctive, with rufous underparts and wing lining. Chin and throat white, face and crown dark, giving it a 'hooded' look. Juvenile could be confused with juvenile Crested Hawk-eagle (see p. 92). Latter has longer tail, its wings are not as broad and it looks slimmer. **HABITAT** Generally seen in good-quality forest patches. **DISTRIBUTION** Can turn up almost anywhere in interior of Sri Lanka away from coast. Most likely to be seen in forest ridges that are close to large areas of forest. **STATUS** UR.

Crested Hawk-eagle
■ *Nisaetus cirrhatus ceylanensis*

DESCRIPTION Medium-sized eagle with pale underparts and crest. Juveniles pale and birds get progressively darker as they age. Adults show a lot of dark streaking on throat and breast. **HABITAT** Forested areas. Often perches on lone trees in open areas, but needs good forest thickets. Varied diet of small animals such as birds, mammals and lizards. **DISTRIBUTION** Throughout Sri Lanka, but most common in dry lowlands. Appears not to occupy as broad a range of disturbed habitats as Crested Serpent-eagle (see p. 86). **VOICE** Whistled sequence of three notes, *whew whe o*. Also longer series of 3–6 notes that ascend as *he he he he*. **STATUS** R.

Mountain (Legge's) Hawk-eagle ■ *Nisaetus nipalensis keelarti*

DESCRIPTION Dark hood and rufous barring distinguish this species from other large eagles. Underneath of tail and flight feathers pale with dark barring, similar to Crested Hawk-eagle (see above) and may be overlooked. In 1878, Legge described the subspecies *keelarti*. Some authors elevated *keelarti* found in Western Ghats and Sri Lanka to species level, but this is not widely accepted. **HABITAT** Forested areas in mountains and mid-hills. Knuckles Wilderness is a reliable site. **DISTRIBUTION** Mid-hills and highlands. **VOICE** High pitched *he-he-he* or *wheuw whe*. Reminiscent of Crested Hawk-eagle (see above). **STATUS** SR. Classified as Vulnerable on IUCN Red List.

Malabar Trogon ■ *Harpactes fasciatus fasciatus*

DESCRIPTION Male has red underparts with white collar separating them from black head. Female has brown head contrasting with underparts that are brownish with hint of orange. Wing-coverts barred with black and white in both sexes. **HABITAT** Good-quality forests in lowlands and hills. Still holds out in secondary-forest fragments close to areas that have been cleared and degraded by farming. **DISTRIBUTION** Throughout Sri Lanka where forest cover is present. Numbers highest in wet zone. **VOICE** Soft, single-noted, repeated *phew* that is lightly sibilant and whistle-like. **STATUS** UR.

LEFT: *Female,* RIGHT: *Male*

Sri Lanka Grey Hornbill ■ *Ocyceros gingalensis* ℮

DESCRIPTION Female has dark mandibles with yellow, crescent-like 'island' on upper mandible. Male has yellow mandibles with dark patch at base of upper mandible. Immature has all-yellow bill. Overall grey upperparts and lack of casque on upper mandible make confusion unlikely with larger Malabar Pied Hornbill (see p. 94). **HABITAT** Found in almost every sizeable forest patch in lowlands and hills. **DISTRIBUTION** Widespread in all but highest mountains. **VOICE** Juddering call that rolls for a few seconds. Also a harsh, far-carrying *kraaa* contact call. **STATUS** E. The more widespread of the two hornbill species found in Sri Lanka.

LEFT: *Female,* RIGHT: *Male*

Malabar Pied Hornbill ■ *Anthracoceros coronatus*

DESCRIPTION Large black-and-white bird with enormous bill. Female has pale area around eye and lacks dark lining on rear of casque. Both sexes have black and pale area at

base of lower mandible. **HABITAT** Areas of large forest with old trees, in dry lowlands. Mainly frugivorous, but also eats small animals when it can. Dependent on old forests for nest sites. **DISTRIBUTION** Widespread in dry lowlands. Absent from the Northern Peninsula. **VOICE** Call raucous and far carrying. Single bird calling gives impression of flock engaged in squabble. **STATUS** R.

LEFT: *Male*, RIGHT: *Female*

Common Hoopoe ■ *Upupa epops ceylonensis*

DESCRIPTION Striking bird with wings and tail boldly barred in black and white. Long, pointed bill slightly downcurved. Body orange and head with crest. **HABITAT** Uncommon bird best encountered in scrub forests in national parks in dry zone. **DISTRIBUTION** Throughout lowlands, especially in dry zone. **VOICE** Call an onomatopoeic *hoopoe*, but most often sounds like an *oop oop*. **STATUS** UR.

Little Green Bee-eater
■ *Merops orientalis orientalis*

DESCRIPTION Black bill forms continuous black line passing through eye to ear-coverts. This characteristic and middle-tail streamers shared with Blue-tailed Bee-eater (see below), with which confusion is possible. Blue-tailed has 'tricolour' pattern below black eye-to-ear line, with thin blue line separated by yellow and buffy-chestnut areas. 'Blue tail', if seen, also separates larger Blue-tailed from Little Green. Adult Little Green has greenish-blue throat demarcated at bottom with thin black line. Juveniles have green throats. Often perches low. **HABITAT** Scrub forest bordering open areas. Like all bee-eaters takes insects on the wing. **DISTRIBUTION** Dry lowlands. **VOICE** Shrill *chirp*, sharper in tone than that of other bee-eaters. **STATUS** R.

Blue-tailed Bee-eater ■ *Merops philippinus philippinus*

DESCRIPTION Large size and blue tail with elongated central feathers. See also details under Little Green Bee-eater (above). **HABITAT** Chooses tall perches, be it trees or TV aerials in cities. Prefers to hunt over open spaces such as paddy fields or scrub forest bordering grassland. Exceptionally, in cities hunts at a good height over roof level, taking insects on the wing. **DISTRIBUTION** Throughout Sri Lanka. **VOICE** Call a cheerful twittering, uttered at rest and in flight. **STATUS** CM.

European Bee-eater

■ *Merops apiaster*

DESCRIPTION Blue underparts and extensive chestnut on wings distinguish this species from Chestnut-headed Bee-eater (see below). Crown and back of head chestnut in both species. Chestnut-headed has blue rump but lacks blue underparts. The European also has extensive chestnut on the shoulder area of the wing. In the Chestnut-headed, the chestnut areas are confined to the crown and mantle. **HABITAT** Forests bordering open areas. **DISTRIBUTION** In the last few years flocks have been recorded in Yala National Park. **VOICE** Rapidly repeated, quivering *peek peek* notes. **STATUS** SM.

Chestnut-headed Bee-eater ■ *Merops leschenaulti leschenaulti*

DESCRIPTION Blue rump in flight. Lacks elongated central-tail feathers found in other bee-eaters recorded in Sri Lanka. Migrant European Bee-eater (see above) has blue underparts. **HABITAT** Forest patches. Perches at mid-level of trees. **DISTRIBUTION**

Throughout lowlands to mid-hills. Low in numbers and not seen in big flocks like other three bee-eaters occurring in Sri Lanka. Unlike the Little Green Bee-eater (see p. 95) this species is just as likely to be seen in the wet zone as in the dry. It has adapted to degraded habitats and can be seen where pockets of forest are mixed with rubber plantations. **VOICE** Tremulous *wheow wheeow* similar to Blue-tailed Bee-eater's (see p. 101). **STATUS** UR.

Indian Roller ■ *Coracias benghalensis indica*

DESCRIPTION At rest, brown mantle feathers can give bird a dull appearance when viewed from back. Strikingly blue-banded upper wings in flight. **HABITAT** Open areas in lowlands. Feeds mainly on insects taken on the wing. Often hawks for insects that take flight when a forest is burnt. **DISTRIBUTION** Mainly lowlands; most common in dry lowlands. Thinly distributed in mid-hills. **VOICE** At times utters a series of repeated, loud, monotonous, metallic *chak* notes. Also some harsh, quarrelsome-sounding notes, especially when interacting with another roller. Juveniles make a harsh *kaaa* reminiscent of a violently angry cat. **STATUS** R.

Common Kingfisher ■ *Alcedo atthis taprobana*

DESCRIPTION Both mandibles in male are black; female has orange on most of lower mandible. Orange ear-coverts diagnostic and distinguish this species from **Blue-eared Kingfisher** *Alcedo meninting*. Lighter, bright blue stripe runs along back. **HABITAT** Widespread in lowlands and hills. Never far from water and predominantly feeds on small fish, but also takes other aquatic animals, including small crabs, amphibians and similar. **DISTRIBUTION** Widespread, from lowlands to highlands. **VOICE** High-pitched, metallic, repeated *tee tee* call, varying a little in pitch. Call often announces its arrival; a tiny blue dart skimming over the water. **STATUS** R.

Male

Black-backed Dwarf Kingfisher ■ *Ceyx erithaca erithacus*

DESCRIPTION Distinctive small kingfisher with orange body and blackish-blue wings. Easily overlooked because of small size (sparrow sized) and discreet habits. Its presence is best noted from its call. **HABITAT** Forested streams in lowlands up to mid-hills. **DISTRIBUTION** From lowlands to mid-hills. **VOICE** Thin, whistled *hee hee*, similar to Common Kingfisher's (see p. 97). **STATUS** UR.

Lesser Pied Kingfisher ■ *Ceryle rudis leucomelanura*

DESCRIPTION Black-and-white kingfisher with habit of hovering over water. Female has single breast-band; male has two. Black bill and crest. **HABITAT** Prefers brackish

water habitats in coastal areas such as lagoons and estuaries. Also found in freshwater marshes and rivers. Abundant in mangrove habitats such as the Muthurajawela marshes north of Colombo. **DISTRIBUTION** Throughout lowlands, but most common close to coastal strip. Occasionally birds visit or are resident in freshwater marshes and lakes in interior. **VOICE** Chirruping call similar to that of a tern. **STATUS** UR.

Male

Stork-billed Kingfisher ■ *Pelargopsis capensis capensis*

DESCRIPTION Large kingfisher with large red, dagger-like bill. Yellowish-buff body, pale chocolate-brown crown, and blue wings, mantle and tail. **HABITAT** Riverine habitats

and freshwater lakes in lowlands and hills. In cities like Colombo, which have many aquatic habitats in the suburbs, may visit gardens and take invertebrates and small reptiles, but preferred habitat is by water. **DISTRIBUTION** Widespread up to mid-hills. **VOICE** Rising *kee kee* changing into mournful wailing series of notes followed by laughing calls. **STATUS** UR.

White-throated Kingfisher ■ *Halcyon smyrnensis fusca*

DESCRIPTION White throat and breast contrast strongly with chocolate-brown underparts and head. Red bill and blue upperparts with chocolate-brown wing-coverts.

In flight shows white patches formed by bases to primaries. **HABITAT** Often seen on telegraph wires over paddy fields. Hunts invertebrates, which form bulk of diet. Does take fish but is more of a forest kingfisher. **DISTRIBUTION** Throughout Sri Lanka from lowlands to highlands. Invertebrate diet brings it to gardens even in Colombo. **VOICE** In flight, harsh, repeated *kra kra*; whinnying call at rest. Nasal chink also uttered from perch. **STATUS** CR.

Black-capped Kingfisher
■ *Halcyon pileata*

DESCRIPTION Black cap, broad white collar, purple upperparts and orange underparts. Bill red, wing-coverts black. Unlikely to be confused with White-throated Kingfisher (see p. 99), which is in the same genus. **HABITAT** Rivers, lagoons and mangrove habitats in lowlands. One bird took up residence by a bridge on the busy A2 near Kalutara; another visited Uda Walawe National Park for at least three consecutive years. **DISTRIBUTION** Recorded mainly in lowlands. **VOICE** Similar to that of White-throated, but calls are deeper. **STATUS** SM.

Brown-headed Barbet ■ *Psilopogon zeylanica zeylanica*

DESCRIPTION Largest of the barbets in Sri Lanka, with brown head, orange-red beak

and facial patch, and green body. Confusion unlikely with any other species. **HABITAT** Well-wooded gardens and village-garden habitats in lowlands and hills. **DISTRIBUTION** From lowlands to higher hills; absent only in highest mountains. **VOICE** Varied. Most regular call a repeated *turrok turrok*, which can start with a roll. Also a nasal call reminiscent of that of **Black-headed Oriole** *Oriolus xanthornus*. **STATUS** CR.

Yellow-fronted Barbet ■ *Psilopogon flavifrons* ℮

DESCRIPTION Like in all the local barbets, body is green. Yellow forehead and blue on face. Confusion with other species unlikely. **HABITAT** Lowlands and hills. In heavy forest this species displaces Brown-headed Barbet (see opposite). **DISTRIBUTION** Mainly wet zone from lowlands to highlands. In lowlands prefers areas with good forest and those with hilly aspects. The most common barbet in highlands. **VOICE** Utters two calls regularly. One is a repeated, tremulous *trokur trokur*. Other begins with a roll (similar to one of calls of Brown-headed), and continues as a repeated, monosyllabic *whurr whurr whurr*. **STATUS** E.

Sri Lanka Small Barbet ■ *Psilopogon rubricapillus* ℮

DESCRIPTION The easiest way to tell this species apart from Coppersmith Barbet (see p. 102) is by the call, described below. Superficially similar to Coppersmith, but this has yellow underparts streaked with dark green. Sri Lanka Small has green underparts lightly streaked with yellow. Both species have red crowns and red necklaces. Coppersmith has yellow on face bordered with dark blue. In Sri Lanka Small, face orange with bright light blue border. **HABITAT** Wooded gardens and forests in lowlands and hills. **DISTRIBUTION** From lowlands to mid-hills. Most common in wet zone. In dry lowlands may be found in riverine forests and areas with good stands of fruiting trees. **VOICE** Repeated *op op op*. Coppersmith has a *tonk tonk tonk*. Both species can occur in the same area and some practice is needed to separate the two calls. **STATUS** CE.

Coppersmith Barbet ■ *Psilopogon haemacephala indica*

DESCRIPTION Can be separated from Sri Lanka Small Barbet (see p. 101) by lemon-yellow, not orange-yellow, patches around eyes, and green-streaked, pale yellowish underparts. **HABITAT** Forested areas in dry lowlands. Occasionally in hills. **DISTRIBUTION** Mainly dry lowlands and lower hills in drier northern and eastern aspects

of central mountains. **VOICE** Monotonous *tonk tonk* as though a copper anvil is being struck by a blacksmith. **STATUS** R.

Greater Sri Lanka Flameback ■ *Chrysocolaptes stricklandi* ⓔ

DESCRIPTION Female's crown black with white flecks. More common Lesser Sri Lanka Flameback (see p. 105) is similar, but this species has an ivory-coloured bill. It also has a

more complex facial pattern, with a white 'island' framed by two thin black moustachial stripes. **HABITAT** Well-wooded gardens and forests in lowlands and hills. Displaces Lesser Sri Lanka in heavily forested patches. **DISTRIBUTION** Absent from arid zones in north-west, north and south-west. Otherwise found in forested areas up to highest mountains. Prefers forests and is absent from urban habitats in which Lesser Sri Lanka is prevalent. **VOICE** Call a repeated, whinnying *tree tree tree tree*. Does not have raucous, ringing insistence of Lesser Sri Lanka's urgent-sounding call. Shrill, whinnying call also used in flight. **STATUS** E.

Female   *Male*

White-naped Flameback
■ *Chrysocolaptes festivus tantus*

DESCRIPTION Forecrown of female speckled black and white. **HABITAT** Wooded areas in dry lowlands. **DISTRIBUTION** Mainly the North-Central Province and south-east from around Hambantota to Yala. **VOICE** Contact calls tremulous, very reminiscent of those of Lesser Sri Lanka Flameback (see p. 105), but not as loud and grating, and much shorter in duration. **STATUS** SR. Classified as Vulnerable on IUCN Red List.

Female   *Male*

Yellow-crowned Woodpecker ■ *Dendrocopos mahrattensis mahrattensis*

DESCRIPTION Overall black-and-white barred, small woodpecker. May be confused with diminutive **Brown-capped Pygmy Woodpecker** *Dendrocopos nanus*, which is much smaller and has a broad dark stripe from eye to shoulder. Male has yellow crown with red at rear. Female's crown all yellow without any red. **HABITAT** Mainly in scrub forests of dry lowlands. **DISTRIBUTION** Confined to dry zone in lowlands. **VOICE** Metallic, slightly tremulous *tleep tleep*. **STATUS** UR. Classified as Vulnerable on IUCN Red List.

Male

Female

Lesser Yellownape
■ *Picus chlorolophus wellsi*

DESCRIPTION Green woodpecker with yellow nape in both sexes. Confusion possible with **Streak-throated Woodpecker** *Picus xanthopygaeus*, but this lacks yellow nape and is streaked rather than barred underneath. Both sexes have red crowns, but female lacks red moustachial stripe of male. (It is unusual in woodpeckers for both sexes to have red on the crown.) **HABITAT** Well-wooded gardens and forests in lowlands and hills. Found only in village gardens where suitable forest patches occur nearby. **DISTRIBUTION** Confined to wet zone in lowlands and mid-hills. **VOICE** Shrill, wheezy, whistled *wheeuw.* **STATUS** R.

Male

Black-rumped Flameback
■ *Dinopium benghalense jaffnense*

DESCRIPTION Female's crown black flecked with white; male's crown red. This species and Lesser Sri Lanka Flameback (see opposite) are easily told apart by the golden and red upperparts respectively. Until 2014 they were treated as 'red-backed' and 'golden-backed' subspecies of the same woodpecker. **HABITAT** Often encountered in coconut plantations. **DISTRIBUTION** Black-rumped replaces Lesser Sri Lanka in northern parts of Sri Lanka from around Puttalam to the Jaffna Peninsula. Black-rumped has very restricted distribution, whereas Lesser Sri Lanka is widespread elsewhere. There is a narrow hybridization zone where the two species meet. **VOICE** Short, sharp, whinnying scream. **STATUS** UR.

Lesser Sri Lanka Flameback ▪ *Dinopium psarodes* ℯ

DESCRIPTION The Black-rumped Flameback (see opposite) was treated as having four subspecies on the Asian mainland and two subspecies in Sri Lanka. Puzzlingly, one of the races in Sri Lanka, the race *psarodes*, had a red back. Since 2014, the southern race *psarodes* has been recognized as a different species, the Lesser Sri Lanka Flameback. The 'golden-backed' race *jaffnense* is now the sole Sri Lankan subspecies of the Black-rumped. Female's crown black at front; red in male. **HABITAT** Gardens and well-wooded areas in lowlands and hills. **DISTRIBUTION** Widespread throughout Sri Lanka, covering areas where Black-rumped Flameback is absent. Both species can overlap in range and hybridized forms occur. **VOICE** Short, sharp, whinnying scream. **STATUS** CE.

Male

Common Kestrel ▪ *Falco tinnunculus*

DESCRIPTION Three races recorded in Sri Lanka: *F. t. interstinctus* is a highly scarce migrant, *F. t. objurgatus* a highly scarce resident and *F. t. tinnunculus* a migrant. They are not distinguishable in the field. Male has grey head and black-tipped grey tail. Female has rufous tail barred with black. Folded wing-tips of vagrant **Lesser Kestrel** *Falco naumanni* nearly reach tip of tail, and its claws are pale rather than black. Adult male Lesser easier to identify as it has rufous upperparts without black markings. **HABITAT** Open country. Distinctive habit of hovering. **DISTRIBUTION** Migrant race *tinnunculus* spreads throughout Sri Lanka on arrival. **VOICE** Flight call a rapid series of 4–5 *yip yip* notes. **STATUS** HSM, HSR, M.

Female

Shaheen (Peregrine) Falcon
■ *Falco peregrinus*

DESCRIPTION Resident subspecies of **Peregrine Falcon** *Falco peregrinus*. Smaller and darker than Peregrine, with blackish hood and upperparts, yellow legs, yellow cere and broad yellow eye-ring. Unlike smaller **Oriental Hobby** *Falco severus*, has rufous underwing-coverts with a hint of barring. **HABITAT** Sites such as Sigiriya, Bible Rock and Yapahuwa, where rocky inselbergs allow it to launch into thermals from a height, are reliable locations for it. Sometimes takes up temporary residence in tall buildings in Colombo, which are like artificial vertical rock faces. Preys mainly on birds captured in flight. **DISTRIBUTION** Lowlands and mid-hills, where suitable hunting posts in the form of cliff faces and inselbergs are found. **VOICE** Rapidly repeated single note, loud and medium in pitch. **STATUS** UR. Classified as Vulnerable on IUCN Red List.

Sri Lanka Hanging-parrot ■ *Loriculus beryllinus* ⓔ

DESCRIPTION Small green bird about the size of House Sparrow (see p. 155). Adults have red crown and rump. Male more brightly coloured than female, which only has trace of male's blue throat. Juveniles have green heads without red crowns. In courtship red rump feathers are raised. **HABITAT** Frequents tall forests. Fond of imbibing sap of Kithul trees *Caryota urens*. **DISTRIBUTION** Common in wet zone. Occurs locally in riverine forests in dry zone and certain dry-zone areas such as Gal Oya. **VOICE** Utters three-syllable, sharp, high-pitched call. **STATUS** CE.

Male

Alexandrine Parakeet ■ *Psittacula eupatria eupatria*

DESCRIPTION Heavy red bill and red shoulder-patch distinguish this species from Rose-ringed Parakeet (see below). Large size and proportionately longer tail than other parakeets. Both sexes have large red shoulder-patch. **HABITAT** Widespread in lowlands and hills. Needs tall trees for nest sites. **DISTRIBUTION** Widespread except in highlands. **VOICE** *Kraa* note often uttered in flight deep and different from Rose-ringed's, which sounds noisy. **STATUS** R.

Male

Rose-ringed Parakeet ■ *Psittacula krameri manillensis*

DESCRIPTION Black collar edged with pink in male; no collar in female. **HABITAT** Adaptable bird that thrives in disturbed habitats and cultivated areas. Found in cities, where it excavates nest holes in tall old trees. Readily visits bird tables for food. **DISTRIBUTION** Widespread, especially in lowlands, where it is considered a pest by paddy farmers. **VOICE** Screeching flight call. **STATUS** CR.

Male

Male

Plum-headed Parakeet
■ *Psittacula cyanocepahala cyanocephala*

DESCRIPTION Small size and plum head of male distinctive. Female has all-grey head. Both sexes have small red shoulder-patch. **HABITAT** Usually found near thinly wooded forests adjoining open areas. Feeds on a variety of food, from fruits, nectar and flower buds, to grain. **DISTRIBUTION** Throughout Sri Lanka, but mainly in hills. **VOICE** Sharp *eenk eenk* call often gives its presence away. **STATUS** UR.

Layard's Parakeet ■ *Psittacula calthropae* ℮

DESCRIPTION Female has dark bill; male's bill red tipped with yellow. Also called Emerald-collared Parakeet, although 'emerald collar' not always clear in the field. **HABITAT** Mainly forested areas in dry lowlands. **DISTRIBUTION** Wet zone up to mid-hills. Flocks also found in the Nilgala area. **VOICE** Raucous calls of flocks distinctive. Two types of call used regularly: a *we wik wur, we wik wur* and a shrill, insistent *i-i-i-i-I*. **STATUS** UE.

LEFT: *Male*, RIGHT: *Female*

Indian Pitta ■ *Pitta brachyura brachyura*

DESCRIPTION Green upperparts, red vent and bold black eye-stripe. In flight bases of primaries have prominent white flashes. Typical dumpy profile of a pitta. The only pitta in Sri Lanka. **HABITAT** Gardens and forests. Favours dense undergrowth where it can be seen hopping about. Will fly up and perch in mid-canopy, from where it may call. **DISTRIBUTION** This migrant spreads widely throughout Sri Lanka on arrival. Large numbers must arrive as it is not unusual even in Colombo for people to find exhausted pittas when they arrive. In some years the author has noticed three Indian Pittas taking up residence on an acre of land in Talangama Wetland. **VOICE** Local Sinhala name *Avichchiya* is onomatopoeic. It is also called the Six O'Clock Bird as it calls *avichichiya* predictably at this time at dusk. Also utters a series of harsh scolding calls. **STATUS** M.

Black-hooded Oriole ■ *Oriolus xanthornus*

DESCRIPTION Adults have 'clean' black heads. Body yellow, wings and tail mainly black. Yellow edges to tertials and outer tail. Juveniles have streaky black heads and duller colours. Vagrant **Black-naped** and **European Golden Orioles** *Oriolus chinensis* and *O. oriolus* lack black hood. In Golden black loreal line does not extend beyond eye. In Black-naped thick black line extends from base of bill to nape. **HABITAT** Bird of woodland. Occupies well-wooded gardens even in cities. Omnivorous, feeding on both invertebrates (mainly insects, caterpillars and similar gleaned from trees), as well as fruits. **DISTRIBUTION** Lowlands to mid-hills; absent from highlands. **VOICE** Orioles have a rich vocabulary of calls. Some are harsh and grating, others very musical and fluty. **STATUS** R.

Small Minivet ■ *Pericrocotus cinnamomeus cinnamomeus*

DESCRIPTION Both sexes have orange rumps, sides of tail and wing-patch. In female orange areas more yellowish than in male. In male entire head dark grey; colourful orange breast-band. In female white on throat shades into yellow on underparts. Often in small flocks. **HABITAT** Wooded patches. Partial to riverine vegetation. **DISTRIBUTION** Widespread throughout Sri Lanka. **VOICE** Thin, wispy, high-pitched calls with many notes in sequence that vary in pitch. **STATUS** R.

Male   *Female*

Orange Minivet ■ *Pericrocotus flammeus flammeus*

DESCRIPTION Male glossy black on head and upperparts, with large flash of scarlet on black wings. Confusion unlikely with male Small Minivet (see above), which is grey rather than glossy black. In female Orange black is replaced with grey, and scarlet is replaced with yellow. Throat yellow. Almost always in small flocks that betray their presence with calls as they fly about. Prefers to feed in canopy. Birds seem restless and flocks always seem to be on the move. **HABITAT** Wooded patches. **DISTRIBUTION** Widespread throughout Sri Lanka. **VOICE** Explosive *zeet zeet* calls herald arrival of flock. Complex sequence of whistled notes. **STATUS** R.

LEFT: *Male*, RIGHT: *Female*

Large Cuckooshrike
■ *Coracina macei layardi*

DESCRIPTION Female distinctly barred on underparts; male has faint barring. Females of this species and Black-headed Cuckooshrike (see below) can be told apart by larger size and dark mask over eye of Large Cuckooshrike. Large also has heavier bill and chunkier build. **HABITAT** Prefers well-wooded areas. **DISTRIBUTION** Widespread except in highlands. Although primarily a forest bird, can tolerate degraded habitats and may be seen close to towns. **VOICE** Nasal, repeated, drawn-out note. Loud. **STATUS** UR.

Black-headed Cuckooshrike ■ *Lalage melanoptera*

DESCRIPTION Female lacks black head and is white below with fine grey barring. Male and female have white vents and under-tail coverts. These lack faint barring seen in Large Cuckooshrike (see above). Both sexes have dark flight feathers; black in male, duller in female. **HABITAT** Wooded patches and gardens throughout lowlands and hills. **DISTRIBUTION** Widespread except in highlands. **VOICE** Beautiful musical notes with sequence that seems like a variation of *yip yip yip yee yee yee*. **STATUS** R.

Male

Ashy Woodswallow (Swallowshrike) ■ *Artamus fuscus*

DESCRIPTION Bluish-grey head and upperparts. Underparts dirty white. Broad-based,

conical bill. Wings extend beyond tail, which is not short but lends the appearance of being short because of the long wings. Compact appearance due to stout build, not slim like build of swallows. Bill structure unusual as it suggests a seed-eating bird, for example from sparrow family. Hawks in the air and spends more time in the air than bee-eaters, but less aerial in habits than swifts or swallows. Woodswallows have clearly found an aerial niche between these two groups. **HABITAT** Mainly lowlands. Hawks for insects over paddy fields and grassland, using vantage points like telegraph wires. **DISTRIBUTION** Lowlands and mid-hills. Becomes scarcer with increasing elevation. Flocks seen in wetlands in suburbs of Colombo, which is surprising given that it is not especially common anywhere. **VOICE** Metallic, wheezy, repeated *kreek*. Shorter contact call, *krik*, in flight. **STATUS** UR.

Pied Flycatcher-shrike

■ *Hemipus picatus leggei*

DESCRIPTION Overall impression is of a small black-and-white bird. Dirty-white or greyish underparts with black upperparts. Black wing has prominent white wing-bar. Almost always in small flocks that prefer canopies. Can be overlooked if attention is not paid to the calls. **HABITAT** Well-wooded areas. Visits degraded habitats if they adjoin good patches of forest. **DISTRIBUTION** Throughout Sri Lanka. **VOICE** Pair of trilling notes of medium length, repeated. Trilling call distinctive and unlikely to be confused with calls of other species in Sri Lanka. **STATUS** UR.

Sri Lanka Woodshrike
■ *Tephrodornis affinis* e

DESCRIPTION Sexes similar. Overall greyish or greyish-brown bird with dark mask. Underparts pale, mostly white. Blackish mask bordered by white supercilium above; below is another band of white that lightly contrasts with dirty-white breast, which fades into white belly. **HABITAT** Scrub jungle in dry lowlands. Occupies low canopy and not difficult to see on mature trees around waterholes in Yala. Feeds on insects. **DISTRIBUTION** Mainly dry lowlands, but there is a strip in the wet zone encompassing Meetirigala Forest where it is present. Distribution pattern is curious. **VOICE** Two or three regular calls. Most frequent call a descending *whee whee whee* of 4–5 notes. Another is a lovely musical, whistled call that ends with *peep peep peep*. **STATUS** E.

Common Iora ■ *Aegithina tiphia multicolor*

DESCRIPTION Male in breeding plumage acquires black upperparts and black tail. It is then distinctive from female, which lacks the black. In non-breeding plumage male similar to female, but panel on wings may show more black. **Marshall's Iora** *Aegithina nigrolutea* is found in east; in this species both sexes have white outer-tail feathers and much more white on wings. The author once found several ioras singing close to each other almost as if they were in a lek. **HABITAT** Forests and wooded gardens. **DISTRIBUTION** Widespread from lowlands to mid-hills. Most numerous in dry lowlands. **VOICE** Soulful, long-drawn notes. Voices of this species and Indian Black Robin (see p. 145) are two of the acoustic signatures of the daytime dry lowlands on hot afternoons. **STATUS** R.

LEFT: *Female*, RIGHT: *Male*

White-browed Fantail ■ *Rhipidura aureola compressirostris*

DESCRIPTION Black and white with relatively long 'fan tail'. Prominent white supercilium. The only fantail in Sri Lanka. Planters in highlands used to call this bird the

'drunken piper' on account of its erratic behaviour involving swooping flights. **HABITAT** Forests. Visits gardens in highlands. Feeds on insects and other invertebrates, and will fly onto house verandahs to pick up insects. **DISTRIBUTION** Strangely absent in western lowlands, but occupies wet zone in highlands. Found throughout dry lowlands. **VOICE** Range of melodious calls and plaintive whistled song. **STATUS** R.

Black Drongo ■ *Dicrurus macrocercus minor*

DESCRIPTION White rictal spot near base of bill, but not always apparent. Irides duller

red than in **Ashy Drongo** *Dicrurus leucophaeus*, which has crimson irides. Flight feathers brown. Under-tail coverts white barred with black, but do not always show. **HABITAT** Thorn-scrub pockets in short-cropped grassland. **DISTRIBUTION** North-western quadrant of Sri Lanka. Distribution is curious, almost as if the species was a recent colonist from southern India spreading southwards from the Adam's Bridge connection to India. Common bird in the Deccan Plateau of southern India. **VOICE** Chittering call that is slightly musical. Varied song with harsh *kraa* notes and whistles. **STATUS** UE.

White-bellied Drongo ■ *Dicrurus caerulescens insularis*

DESCRIPTION Overall black drongo with dull red eyes and variable white on belly and vent. Dry-zone race *D. c. insularis* has more white on underparts extending from vent to belly. Wet-zone race *D. c. leucopygialis* has white restricted to vent, but variations with more white are seen. **HABITAT** Forest edges, disturbed habitats and village gardens. Visits gardens in Colombo that adjoin open degraded land or marshland. Generally absent from heavily built-up areas. Feeds on invertebrates taken on the wing or gleaned off plants. **DISTRIBUTION** Dry zone. Two subspecies between them found throughout lowlands and mid-hills. Curiously absent from arid south-eastern corner of Sri Lanka, although migrant Ashy Drongos occupy this area. **VOICE** Sometimes pairs utter whinnying call. Wide repertoire of notes mixed with mimicked sequences of Shikra, Jerdon's Leafbird (see pp. 90 and 149), domestic cats and other animals; include harsh notes, whistles and liquid belling notes. **STATUS** CR.

Greater Racket-tailed Drongo ■ *Dicrurus paradiseus ceylonicus*

DESCRIPTION 'Rackets' on ends of bare outer-tail shafts. Naked tail shafts long in adults. Sri Lanka Crested Drongo (see p. 116) with bare shafts can be confused with this, but in latter lobes at end of tail are turned inwards. In Sri Lanka Crested they are turned outwards. In latter naked shafts are relatively short. Naked shafts in Sri Lanka Crested caused confusion in the past with Greater Racket-tailed's. Identification and consequently distribution of the two species were clarified by local ornithologist Deepal Warakagoda. Crest on forehead prominent in adults, less obvious in immatures. **HABITAT** Riverine forests of dry zone. **DISTRIBUTION** Restricted to dry and intermediate zone forests. **VOICE** Two-noted call where pitch of notes varies. Complex belling call that is repeated. **STATUS** UR.

Sri Lanka Crested Drongo ▪ *Dicrurus lophorhinus*

DESCRIPTION Crest on forehead and deeply forked tail with lobes facing outwards. Tail usually without rackets, but see notes under Greater Racket-tailed Drongo (p. 115) for confusion with birds that have bare shafts. Crest, a tuft-like projection on forehead, only obvious at close quarters. **HABITAT** Good-quality forests in wet lowlands. Still present in rainforest pockets such as Bodhinagala. **DISTRIBUTION** Restricted to lowlands to mid-elevation wet-zone forests. **VOICE** Lovely repertoire of belling calls. May continue calling at times for relatively long period. Also a great mimic. **STATUS** UE.

Asian (Indian) Paradise Flycatcher ▪ *Terpsiphone paradisi paradisi*

DESCRIPTION Two subspecies occur in Sri Lanka, resident race *T. p. ceylonensis* (see opposite) and migrant race *T. p. paradisi*. Fully mature adult males easy to tell apart: Indian male black and white; Sri Lanka male has black head, chestnut upperparts and white underparts. Indian males gradually acquire white, from being chestnut in first year. By second year they begin to acquire white feathers and show mix of chestnut and white. By third year male plumage is completely white. Females of the two races are similar and lack tail streamers. **HABITAT** Lowlands and hills in forests and well-wooded gardens. **DISTRIBUTION** Migrant race spreads all over Sri Lanka from lowlands to highlands. Paradise flycatchers seen in cities such as Colombo in west during migrant season are all of this race. **VOICE** Harsh *krik* with nasal intonation, repeated at a few seconds apart, is contact call. Song a beautiful soft melody of various musical notes mixed with some rapid sequences. **STATUS** M.

Male

Asian (Sri Lanka) Paradise Flycatcher
■ *Terpsiphone paradisi ceylonensis*

DESCRIPTION In resident race *T. p. ceylonensis* males are chestnut throughout their lives. See more details under Indian race (opposite). **HABITAT** Lowlands and hills in forests and well-wooded gardens. **DISTRIBUTION** Dry lowlands. **VOICE** As Indian race. **STATUS** R.

LEFT: *Female*, RIGHT: *Male*

Black-naped Blue Monarch ■ *Hypothymis azurea ceylonensis*

DESCRIPTION Habit of actively foraging in mid-canopy and not staying for long helps distinguish this bird from less active and sedentary feeding behaviour of Tickell's Blue Flycatcher (see p. 147), which it superficially resembles. Also makes a sharp *zit* call as it forages. Tickell's has orange-red breast compared with blue of this species. Juvenile monarchs have blue heads, but rest of plumage can look plain grey. **HABITAT** Forests. **DISTRIBUTION** Throughout Sri Lanka up to mid-hills. **VOICE** Explosive *chwizz*, repeated. **STATUS** UR.

Brown Shrike ■ *Lanius cristatus cristatus*

DESCRIPTION Juvenile in particular can have pale brown crown edged pale on sides and with a fairly broad white forehead. Viewed from certain angles, especially from side, whole crown can appear silvery-grey, leading to confusion with **Philippine Shrike** *Lanius*

cristatus. Juveniles show barring on underparts and have broad, pale-edged tertials. Brown Shrikes at different stages of age and moult can look very different. Sometimes they look dull; at other times they show rich orangish-buff on flanks and look richer brown above. **HABITAT** Scrubby areas. **DISTRIBUTION** Spreads throughout Sri Lanka on arrival. **VOICE** Harsh rattle. **STATUS** CM.

Long-tailed Shrike (Rufous-rumped Shrike)
■ *Lanius schach caniceps*

DESCRIPTION Looks similar to **Bay-backed Shrike** *Lanius vittatus* frontally, but has grey not maroon on mantle, and rufous rump. A fairly confiding shrike, allows a close

approach and has become habituated to people. In areas such as Mannar it is not difficult to see this on the sides of the main roads. **HABITAT** Scrub jungle areas. **DISTRIBUTION** Northern parts of Sri Lanka. It is unusual that it has not spread further south given the availability of suitable habitat. **VOICE** Harsh, repeated *kraa*. **STATUS** SR.

Sri Lanka Blue Magpie
■ *Urocissa ornata* (e)

DESCRIPTION Unmistakable bird with chocolate-brown on head and wings, and red bill, eye-ring and legs set against blue plumage. Tail graduated with white edges and white tip. Birds show cooperative nesting behaviour, with younger birds helping adults at nest. Has become habituated in Sinharaja since the 1980s, and many people can now enjoy close views of it. HABITAT Restricted to wet-zone forests of fairly significant size. DISTRIBUTION Wet zone from lowlands to highlands. VOICE Wide repertoire of calls, most of which are harsh and grating, and some that have metallic intonations. STATUS UE. Classified as Vulnerable on IUCN Red List.

House Crow ■ *Corvus splendens protegatus*

DESCRIPTION Can be distinguished from bigger Indian Jungle Crow (see p. 120) by its grey nape; in fact one of its older names is Grey-necked Crow. More elegant crow than chunky Indian Jungle Crow. HABITAT Has adapted well to presence of humans, so much so that it is almost entirely absent from habitats that lack human presence or are human modified. DISTRIBUTION Widespread; in forests replaced by Indian Jungle. VOICE Harsh *kaaa kaa*, which gave rise to the Sinhalese onomatopoeic name *Kakkaa*. STATUS CR.

Indian Jungle Crow ■ *Corvus macrorhynchos*

DESCRIPTION Chunky, uniformly glossy black. Large bill only evident in comparisons with House Crow (see p. 119), as all crows have heavy bills. **HABITAT** Alternative name

Jungle Crow betrays that it can be seen in natural habitats where presence of humans is not evident. Co-mingles with House Crow in urban areas. **DISTRIBUTION** Widespread; not as abundant as House Crow. **VOICE** Deep-throated, repeated *kraa*. Much deeper voice than House Crow's. **STATUS** R.

Grey-headed Canary-flycatcher ■ *Culicicapa ceylonensis ceylonensis*

DESCRIPTION Sparrow-sized bird with grey head and breast, olive-yellow above and brighter yellow below. Confiding bird that will perch in view and allow a close approach. **HABITAT** Hills and highlands. Forests and gardens. **DISTRIBUTION** Main range in highlands, where it is a common bird in cloud forests. Garden bird in cities such as Nuwara

Eliy, but this may be because this is a cloud-forest city, set within a bowl surrounded by cloud forests. **VOICE** Machine-gun like, chattering call similar to call of a canary, hence the name canary-flycatcher. **STATUS** UR.

Great Tit ■ *Parus major mahrattarum*

DESCRIPTION Black head with bold white cheek-patch, and grey upperparts with prominent white wing-bar. Black chin and throat. Dark line runs through middle of belly to vent – thicker and clearer in male than in female. A greyer subspecies of familiar Great Tit of Europe. Has been treated as **Cinereous Tit** *Parus cinereous* by some authors but treated by others as subspecies *mahrattarum* of Great Tit. Forty-three subspecies of Great Tit have been described and fall within four groups, with *major* in the Palearctic and *cinereous* from Southwest Asia, the Indian subcontinent to Indochina and Indonesia. **HABITAT** Visits gardens in hills and highlands. **DISTRIBUTION** Throughout Sri Lanka. Common garden bird in highlands. In dry lowlands more likely to be seen in tall forests along rivers. **VOICE** Contact call a rattling *churr*. Regularly used three-note contact call is *chee chee choo-wit*. Wide range of vocalizations, including far-carrying *teacher teacher* call. **STATUS** R.

Jerdon's Bushlark ■ *Mirafra affinis ceylonensis*

DESCRIPTION Similar to Oriental Skylark (see p. 122). Shorter, chunky bill helps to separate it from the slimmer, longer-billed pipits. At times face is chestnut bordered by clear white supercilium on top and white margin at back of cheek. Most of the time cheek is streaked. Shorter tail also separates it from pipits. Rufous on wing does not show well when bird is at rest. Also known as Rufous-winged Bushlark. **HABITAT** Open areas in dry lowlands. **DISTRIBUTION** Dry lowlands. **VOICE** Series of thin, wispy, ascending *tseep tseep* notes. In courtship the bird rises and ascends while singing, then makes a 'parachute descent'. **STATUS** R.

Ashy-crowned Sparrow-lark ▪ *Eremopterix griseus*

DESCRIPTION Female is a drab, sparrow-like bird, but lacks chestnut flight feathers of female House Sparrow and has a weaker bill. Males have blackish throats. Males in breeding plumage are striking, with black underparts, white face and black line from base of beak to neck. **HABITAT** Open areas in dry lowlands. Almost entirely ground dwelling. **DISTRIBUTION** Dry lowlands. In December 2003 a tired female was photographed in Horton Plains National Park. It may have been from a flock that was travelling locally, or perhaps a migrant bird from Asia that was flying over the mountains to reach the south. It is likely that many species considered to be resident are actually supplemented with wintering populations.

VOICE Song has long trilling notes sounding like a fishing line being drawn in; also some long-drawn, single *whee* notes. **STATUS** UR.

LEFT: *Male*, RIGHT: *Female*

Oriental Skylark ▪ *Alauda gulgula*

DESCRIPTION Both Jerdon's Bushlark (see p. 121) and this species have well-marked ear-coverts. In Jerdon's Bushlark rufous flight feathers do not show at rest. Confusion is likely between the two species at rest. Skylark has finer bill than Jerdon's Bushlark and is chunkier in build than Paddyfield Pipit (see p. 158), with which confusion is also possible. Skylark often raises crest of feathers on crown. **HABITAT** Open areas in dry lowlands and hills. Most prevalent in arid habitats. Skies in area around Mannar are full of this skylark's song. **DISTRIBUTION** Arid south-east extending along east coast to dry lowlands from the North-Central Plains to the Northern Peninsula. **VOICE** Series of *chee chee* notes interspersed with notes of different pitch, and trills and chirps. There is a pattern to the sequence, which is complex and keeps changing. Singing bird usually ascends the sky as it sings and is easily located. **STATUS** Two resident races described from Sri Lanka: *A. g. gulgula* UR in dry lowlands, and *A. g. australis* SR in higher hills.

Zitting Cisticola

■ *Cisticola juncidis*

DESCRIPTION Warbler of grassland, heavily streaked on crown and upperparts, with white-tipped tail that is fanned out in flight, hence alternative name Fan-tailed Warbler. In short-cropped grassland may scurry about on the ground in mouse-like fashion. **HABITAT** Grassland and paddy fields. **DISTRIBUTION** Widespread throughout Sri Lanka. **VOICE** *Zit zit* call uttered in flight makes this species easy to identify (named after its call). **STATUS** R.

Grey-breasted Prinia ■ *Prinia hodgsonii leggei*

DESCRIPTION Dark grey hood with clean white chin and throat. Male has broad grey breast-band; female's more diffused. White underparts. Red irides gleam through blackish loreal band, which continues through eyes. Unlike other prinias, which are usually seen alone or as a pair, the Grey-breasted is usually seen in a small, noisy flock. **HABITAT** Scrub forest in dry lowlands. Most arboreal of the prinias. Does not need grassland like other prinias, and found in scrub forest as well. Like other prinias and many of the warblers it feeds on invertebrates ranging from eggs and caterpillars to adult insects. Several species of prinia may be found in the same matrix of thorn scrub forest and grassland, a good example of niche partitioning. **DISTRIBUTION** Lowlands to mid-hills. Easiest to see in dry lowlands. **VOICE** Rattly three notes, *zeet zeet zeet*, uttered rapidly and repeated. **STATUS** UR.

Ashy Prinia ■ *Prinia socialis brevicauda*

DESCRIPTION Bluish-grey upperparts; underparts tinged orange, paler on throat.

Pale-tipped tail has black subterminal band. Female develops white supercilium in front of eye in breeding season. Reddish irides. HABITAT Lowland grassland, but most common in patanas in hills. Can occur close to urban habitats. Next to Plain Prinia (see opposite), the most resilient prinia to urbanization. DISTRIBUTION Throughout Sri Lanka. VOICE Clear, repeated *chewok chewok*. Sometimes higher pitched, repeated notes are introduced. STATUS R.

Jungle Prinia ■ *Prinia sylvatica valida*

DESCRIPTION Diffused supercilium does not extend behind eye in male. Supercilium in both sexes less distinct than in Plain Prinia (see opposite). In breeding season female's supercilium extends behind eye. Stouter bill (dark in male) also distinguishes this species

from Plain. Reddish irides, black pupils. Calls of the prinia species are different from each other. HABITAT Scrub jungle in dry lowlands. DISTRIBUTION Suitable habitat throughout Sri Lanka except in highlands. Dry lowlands offer best chance of seeing this bird. VOICE Loud, repeated *tcheoow* note. Repeated note strongly articulated, as if each note is thrown out with some force. STATUS R.

Plain Prinia
■ *Prinia inornata insularis*

DESCRIPTION Distinct, broad pale supercilium. Overall pale sandy-brown; much paler underneath, appearing almost white at times. Black bill. **HABITAT** Lowland grassland. It occasionally can be seen foraging in thick hedgerows bordering paddy fields and other grassland habitats. But open grasslands are a mandatory requirement for this prinia. **DISTRIBUTION** Widespread throughout Sri Lanka. Most tolerant of all the prinias to urbanization. Still to be found close to Colombo in the Kotte marshes and Talangama Wetland. **VOICE** Range of cheerful vocalizations, typically *tleep tleep* with higher pitched notes at end of a sequence. **STATUS** R.

Common Tailorbird ■ *Orthotomus sutorius*

DESCRIPTION Green upperparts, white underparts, long tail and rusty crown. Fine, downcurved bill. Very different in appearance and behaviour from other members of its family. Female lacks extended central feathers. Jerky movements; very vocal. Named for nest it stitches together, encased between two or more leaves it has sewn together. **HABITAT** Disturbed habitats, hedgerows and gardens. **DISTRIBUTION** Widespread throughout Sri Lanka; common garden bird. **VOICE** Can include *yip yip* notes alternating with *pik pik*, then *tchewk tchewk* and variations. However, generally a note is repeated a few times before switching to another. **STATUS** CR.

Blyth's Reed Warbler ■ *Acrocephalus dumetorum*

DESCRIPTION Plain brown upperparts and fairly well-defined supercilium. Best located and identified by *chakking* call. Furtive bird, keeping well within shrubby thickets as it forages. Resident **Indian Reed Warbler** *Acrocephalus stentoreus* occupies wetland reed habitats and has different vocalizations. It is longer tailed and more likely to show itself. **HABITAT** Shrubby vegetation. **DISTRIBUTION** Throughout Sri Lanka. **VOICE** Constant *chak chak* notes help to confirm its identity. **STATUS** CM.

Sri Lanka Bush Warbler
■ *Elaphrornis palliseri* **e**

DESCRIPTION Dark warbler with skulking habits; keeps close to forest floor. Male has red irides; female's are buff. **HABITAT** Thickets in highland forests. **DISTRIBUTION** Nillu undergrowth in forests around Nuwara Eliya. Horton Plains is a reliable place to spot it. **VOICE** Pairs often keep in touch using a series of nasal *tszip tszip* contact calls. **STATUS** UE. Classified as Endangered on IUCN Red List.

Female

Barn Swallow ■ *Hirundo rustica*

DESCRIPTION European race *H. r. rustica* has complete black breast-band. Asian race *H. r. gutturalis* has incomplete breast-band and is the most common subspecies. Race *H. r. tytleri*, also known as Tytler's Swallow, suffused with pink on underparts; some individuals in other two races may also be tinged pink on underparts.

HABITAT Hunts over open areas, using tall trees and telephone lines as perches. **DISTRIBUTION** Spreads throughout Sri Lanka up to highlands. Before departure large flocks gather in lowlands; especially visible in southern coastal strip near Bundala National Park. **VOICE** Metallic chirping notes with trill at end of sequence, which is repeated. **STATUS** Race *gutturalis* CM; *rustica* UM; *tytleri* SM.

Juvenile

House or Hill Swallow ■ *Hirundo javanica*

DESCRIPTION Dirty-white underparts. No black breast-band. Tail forked as in migrant Barn Swallow (see above), but lacks long outer-tail streamers. **HABITAT** Hills and highlands. Will nest in buildings. **DISTRIBUTION** Mainly wet zone up to highlands. Becomes more common with increasing elevation. **VOICE** Soft chittering calls at rest and in flight. **STATUS** R.

Indian Red-rumped Swallow ■ *Hirundo daurica erythropygia*

DESCRIPTION One of several subspecies of widespread **Red-rumped Swallow** *Hirundo daurica*. Indian race has finer streaking than Nepali race *H. d. nipalensis*, a highly scarce migrant. Underparts much paler than those of Sri Lanka Swallow (see below), once considered to be another race of Red-rumped Swallow. Rump can also look very pale in flight. **HABITAT** Open areas interspersed with forest in dry lowlands. **DISTRIBUTION** Recorded in dry lowlands. Can occur in large flocks. Uda Walawe National Park is one of the best sites to see it. **VOICE** Sounds similar in pattern to Sri Lanka Swallow's, but less liquid in quality. **STATUS** SM.

Sri Lanka Swallow ■ *Cecropsis hyperythra* ⓔ

DESCRIPTION Deep red underparts and rump help separate this species from migrant races of Red-rumped Swallow (see above). **HABITAT** Open habitats such as grassland, coastal areas, paddy fields and similar. **DISTRIBUTION** Throughout Sri Lanka. **VOICE** Call, often uttered in flight, has a liquid bubbling quality to it. **STATUS** E.

Black-capped Bulbul ■ *Pycnonotus melanicterus*

DESCRIPTION Black cap and yellow plumage distinctive. In flight often shows white tips on tail feathers. **HABITAT** Forests in lowlands and hills. **DISTRIBUTION** Mainly wet zone up to mid-hills. Also present in dry-zone forests, but in much lower numbers than in wet-zone forests. **VOICE** Most frequent calls include sequence with *pip pip* notes; another has several grasshopper warbler-like churring notes. Yet another, a song, has a series of rising melancholy syllables. **STATUS** UE.

Red-vented Bulbul ■ *Pycnonotus cafer haemorrhousus*

DESCRIPTION Greyish-brown bulbul with pale edges to feathers giving a scalloped look. Head black; dusky breast shading to white; ends in bright red vent. Tail tipped with white. **HABITAT** Variety of habitats from scrubland to home gardens. Found even in major cities such as Colombo. **DISTRIBUTION** Widespread throughout Sri Lanka. One of the most common birds in Sri Lanka. **VOICE** Tremulous two-note call that sounds like '*teacher bread*' and at times '*pitta bread*'. In the evenings utters churring noise. **STATUS** CR.

Yellow-eared Bulbul
■ *Pycnonotus penicillatus* ℮

DESCRIPTION Face strikingly patterned in black and white with yellow ear-tufts. Inner webs of flight feathers leaden in colour; outer webs green. Most of the time only green shows, and body looks olive-green and yellow. **HABITAT** Hills and highlands. Visits gardens in highlands. **DISTRIBUTION** In wet zone from mid-hills to highlands. Becomes more common with increasing elevations. **VOICE** Draws attention to itself with loud *pik pik pik* calls. Call also uttered in flight. Additionally has a guttural call. **STATUS** E. Classified as Vulnerable on IUCN Red List.

White-browed Bulbul ■ *Pycnonotus luteolus insulae*

DESCRIPTION Nondescript brown bulbul with pale brown upperparts and dirty-white underparts. White eyebrow distinct most of the time. Yellow malar stripe and vent. Can be

discreet in behaviour – presence is picked out by call. **HABITAT** Forests and well-wooded gardens in lowlands and hills. **DISTRIBUTION** Throughout Sri Lanka except in highlands. **VOICE** Uplifting *chik-chee-chee-chik-chik* followed immediately by two grating notes and musical chirps. Complex call sequence. **STATUS** R.

Yellow-browed Bulbul
■ *Acritillas indica*

DESCRIPTION Overall yellow bulbul; more yellow on underparts and olive-yellow on upperparts. Yellow encircles eye and runs from bill-base to eye. **HABITAT** Forest patches, mainly in wet lowlands. **DISTRIBUTION** From lowlands to mid-hills. Two races, *I. i. guglielmi* and *I. i. indica*, are described from wet zone and dry zone, but are indistinguishable in the field. Dry-zone race scarce. Most likely to be seen in wet-zone forests and adjoining village gardens. **VOICE** Characteristic *quick quick* call. **STATUS** UR.

Square-tailed Black Bulbul ■ *Hypsipetes ganeesa*

DESCRIPTION Black bulbul with long, pointed red bill and red legs. Frequents tree canopy, from which it calls noisily. **HABITAT** Forest patches in lowlands. **DISTRIBUTION** Mainly wet lowlands, but locally found in dry-zone riverine forests. **VOICE** Loud, tremulous *chik-chuo*. Also series of wailing calls interspersed with indignant chattering notes. **STATUS** UR.

Green or Bright-green Warbler ■ *Phylloscopus nitidus*

DESCRIPTION Similar to scarce **Greenish Warbler** *Phylloscopus trochiloides*, but with strong hint of yellow on underparts. Yellow wash reduces in worn adults. **HABITAT** Where there is adequate forest cover. Keeps mainly to canopy level on trees. **DISTRIBUTION** Throughout Sri Lanka. More abundant than Large-billed Leaf Warbler (see below). **VOICE** Easily located by *thirrip* call. **STATUS** CM.

Large-billed Leaf Warbler ■ *Phylloscopus magnirostris*

DESCRIPTION Dark eye-line and sharply defined supercilium against dark crown. Bill larger than Bright-green Warbler's (see above), but not as apparent in the field. Calls are the best way of distinguishing the two species. **HABITAT** Forests and well-wooded patches and gardens. **DISTRIBUTION** Throughout Sri Lanka. Absent from cities such as Colombo, so may need forest canopy formed of native trees. **VOICE** Calls important for distinguishing leaf warblers. Call thin and structure roughly of form *hi-hee-hi*, repeated in variations of pitch. Song musical and of form *whi-we-weee-we-wee*, which is repeated. **STATUS** CM.

Sri Lanka White-eye ■ *Zosterops ceylonensis* ℮

DESCRIPTION Wider 'split' in white eye-ring in front of eye than in Oriental White-eye (see below). Also darker and slightly larger than Oriental. Calls of the two species very different from each other. **HABITAT** Forests and wooded gardens. **DISTRIBUTION** Mainly highlands; occasional movements to lowland wet zone (for example Sinharaja), where it mixes with Oriental. **VOICE** Sri Lanka's calls much louder than those of Oriental. Flocks utter chirping calls to stay in contact. Also a call of rapid sequence of *tchew tchew* notes that are drummed out. **STATUS** E.

Oriental White-eye ■ *Zosterops palpebrosus egregia*

DESCRIPTION Compared with Sri Lanka White-eye (see above), this species has brighter lemon-yellow upperparts, cleaner white underparts and a slimmer build. Calls diagnostic in the field. **HABITAT** Occupies mid-storey and canopies of small trees. **DISTRIBUTION** Throughout Sri Lanka. Most common in lowlands and hills, but can ascend to highlands. **VOICE** Song a sequence of 6–7 complex notes. Birds keep in contact with a series of soft, chattering calls. **STATUS** R.

Ashy-headed Laughingthrush ■ *Garrulax cinereifrons* ℮

DESCRIPTION Brown body and bluish rather than ashy head that may not be noticed unless a good view is had. Typically forages near the ground and may be missed in a Sinharaja bird wave unless you are alert to its calls. **HABITAT** Confined to extensive lowland rainforests. **DISTRIBUTION** Flocks most habituated in Sinharaja and permit good views, especially on the rare occasions when they explore mid-levels of canopies or come out to feed on Bovitiya bushes. 'Barrier Gate' flock at Sinharaja offers a good chance to see this bird. **VOICE** Flocks keep up medley of hysterical-sounding calls, sometimes with a faint metallic quality. **STATUS** SE. Classified as Endangered on IUCN Red List.

Sri Lanka Scimitar-babbler ■ *Pomatorhinus melanurus* ℮

DESCRIPTION Prominent white eyebrow, black mask through eye and downcurved

'scimitar' bill help to identify this species. Dark brown upperparts contrast with white underparts. **HABITAT** Prefers areas of good forest. Found in village-garden habitats where areas of forest adjoin them. **DISTRIBUTION** Both lowland wet zone and dry zone, ascending to highlands. However, in dry zone absent from thorn-scrub forest. **VOICE** Almost always seen in duetting pairs: male utters a long, bubbling series of calls that end with a *kriek* from female. Song so well synchronized that sound often appears to come from a single bird. **STATUS** E.

Dark-fronted Babbler ■ *Rhopocichla atriceps*

DESCRIPTION Small babbler, quite different in shape from larger babblers because it has a short tail. 'Highwayman's' black mask, white eye-ring and pale bill lend it a distinctive look. **HABITAT** Prefers large forested areas, but even as recently as 2014 a small flock was holding out in the One Acre Reserve in Talangama on the outskirts of Colombo. This is, however, atypical and the birds need to be close to forest patches. **DISTRIBUTION** Throughout Sri Lanka. A flock seems to follow every Sinharaja bird wave; these babblers hold territories and join a feeding flock as it sweeps through. **VOICE** Small flocks keep in touch with a *prruk prruk* chattering call. **STATUS** R.

Yellow-eyed Babbler ■ *Chrysomma sinense nasale*

DESCRIPTION Looks like a 'misfit' in babbler family, with its broad-based, short, stubby black bill. Orange-red eye-ring bordered with yellow, surrounded by white face except for brown cheeks. Brown upperparts, white underparts and yellow legs. Usually in pairs. **HABITAT** Tall grassland and scrub. **DISTRIBUTION** Suitable habitats throughout Sri Lanka except in highlands. Most prevalent in dry lowlands. **VOICE** Musical song quite unlike that of other babbler species. Liquid-like, fluty notes. **STATUS** R.

Orange-billed or Sri Lanka Rufous Babbler
■ *Turdoides rufescens* (e)

DESCRIPTION Orange bill and legs, rufous body and constant chattering help to distinguish this species from other babblers. **HABITAT** Rainforests mainly in lowlands, but also in highlands. Tends to be found only where extensive forests remain. **DISTRIBUTION** Wet zone. Almost absent from extensive but heavily disturbed Kanneliya Rainforest. Its near absence is a mystery. In sites such as Kithulgala forages in disturbed habitats, but always within a short flight from good-quality forest. **VOICE** Chattering calls. Familiar sound in large lowland rainforests such as Sinharaja as it is a key nucleus species of the Sinharaja bird wave. **STATUS** UE.

Yellow-billed Babbler ■ *Turdoides affinis taprobanus*

DESCRIPTION Sandy-brown, almost grey babbler that is highly vocal and gregarious.

Yellow bill, facial skin and legs on otherwise fairly uniform colour scheme. **HABITAT** Grassland and scrub in dry lowlands. Has adapted to home gardens. **DISTRIBUTION** Widespread. There is no nook or corner in Sri Lanka that this babbler does not occupy, other than where high-rise buildings leave it without tree cover. **VOICE** High-pitched, chattering calls. Uttered at slow pace when birds are foraging; reaches a high frequency and sounds hysterical when they are interacting. **STATUS** CR.

Brown-capped Babbler ■ *Pellorneum fuscocapillus* ⓔ

DESCRIPTION Small brown babbler with darker brown cap. Very shy and keeps hidden. In Sinharaja has become more habituated, and in the evenings pairs may come out on to the road. **HABITAT** Remaining forest patches. **DISTRIBUTION** Throughout Sri Lanka up to highlands. Widespread bird whose call can be heard from every forested thicket. **VOICE** Distinctive *pritee dear* betrays presence of bird, which is a great skulker, rarely showing itself in the open. Beautiful song. **STATUS** UE.

Velvet-fronted Nuthatch
■ *Sitta frontalis frontalis*

DESCRIPTION Red bill, black forehead, dark blue upperparts and whitish underparts. Male has thin black line that continues behind eye; absent in female. Sometimes seen in family flocks, but typically adults encountered in pairs. **HABITAT** Tall- and medium-stature forests, where the bird clambers along tree trunks, most times descending head down. Can also position itself upside-down on a horizontal branch and still cling to the tree with its strong claws. Moves in a jerky fashion. **DISTRIBUTION** Throughout Sri Lanka. **VOICE** Loud, quivering *chizzzz* call, made up of a series of machine-gunned *chizz* notes. **STATUS** R.

Female

White-faced Starling ■ *Sturnornis albofrontatus* ℮

DESCRIPTION White on forehead, face, supercilium, chin and throat. White on throat

fades into dirty-white underparts with white streaks. Upperparts steely-grey. Overall impression when seen from below is of a pale bird. **HABITAT** Frequents canopies of rainforests. Rarely seen in mid-canopy unless it has joined a mixed feeding flock. **DISTRIBUTION** Restricted to a few lowland wet-zone forests such as Sinharaja and Kithulgala. Starlings are powerful fliers so may turn up briefly in small pockets of forest in search of food, but it seems that breeding populations are confined only to large tracts of rainforest in lowlands and mid-hills. **VOICE** Whistled, repeated *cheep*, sometimes turning into two-toned *cheep-cheowp*. **STATUS** HSE. Classified as Endangered on IUCN Red List.

Brahminy Starling ■ *Sturnia pagodarum*

DESCRIPTION Colourful starling with black crown and nape, orange-yellow beak with

blue base, greyish upperparts and rufous-orange underparts. Pale, faintly green irides. **HABITAT** Scrub jungle in dry lowlands. **DISTRIBUTION** Distribution unusual for this winter migrant: favours arid zone in south-east and north-west, and generally coastal strip around northern area of Sri Lanka. Given that thorn-scrub habitat is more widely spread, it is not clear why this passerine, which arrives in large numbers, occupies such a small area of dry lowlands. **VOICE** Pleasant song; cackling contact calls. **STATUS** M. Numbers variable from year to year.

Rosy Starling ■ *Pastor roseus*

DESCRIPTION Almost two toned, with black hood extending down to upper breast, rosy underparts and mantle, and black wings. Orange-yellow beak. Should not be confused with Brahminy Starling (see opposite), which does not have black hood and black on wings. Juveniles and first-winter birds (seen in Sri Lanka) pale brown with traces of black plumage of second-year birds. Colours more vivid in breeding plumage. **HABITAT** Scrub jungle in dry lowlands. **DISTRIBUTION** Can spread all over Sri Lanka in some years, but mainly found in dry lowlands. **VOICE** Song a series of chitters and chirps. Contact calls quivering chirps. **STATUS** M. In some years tens of thousands of Rosy Starlings arrive and form huge roosts.

Common Myna ■ *Acridotheres tristis melanosternus*

DESCRIPTION Yellow bill, yellow facial skin behind eye, chocolate-brown upperparts and underparts turning blackish on head. White vent and wing-bar, which also show at rest. In flight wing-tips look like whirr of black and white. **HABITAT** Garden bird that is a ground feeder on short-cropped grass. Will turn over cow dung in search of insects and pull out invertebrates from soft ground. **DISTRIBUTION** Throughout Sri Lanka. **VOICE** Cheeps and chirps interspersed with grunting notes. **STATUS** CR.

Sri Lanka Hill-myna ■ *Gracula ptilogenys* ⓔ

DESCRIPTION Chunkier looking than Southern Hill-myna (see below). Key differences are a single pair of wattles on nape (Southern has extra pair under eye), black-based orange bill (yellow in Southern), and pale greyish irides (brown in Southern). Both species overall glossy black with prominent white wing-bar. **HABITAT** Tree canopies. **DISTRIBUTION** Bird of large and good-quality wet-zone forests from lowlands to higher hills. Sinharaja

and Kithulgala are good locations for this uncommon endemic. **VOICE** Series of sharp, whistled *yowp* and *yeep* calls interspersed with nasal wheezing notes. **STATUS** UE. Classified as Vulnerable on IUCN Red List.

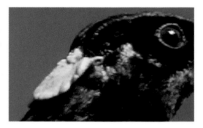

Southern Hill-myna ■ *Gracula indica*

DESCRIPTION All-yellow bill (orange with black base in Sri Lanka Hill-myna, see above). Sri Lanka darker than Southern. Diagnostic feature is two pairs of wattles in Southern, one under eye (missing in Sri Lanka) and one on nape. In juvenile Southern nape wattles develop after those under eyes. **HABITAT** Forests and well-wooded patches. Visits village gardens where there are good-quality forest patches nearby. **DISTRIBUTION** Lowlands and hills in both wet and dry zones. **VOICE** Long, whistled notes separated by distinct interval, with notes alternating in pitch with rising intonation, followed by another with falling intonation, interspersed with nasal sawing notes, *zee-zit*. Calls sound more complex than those of Sri Lanka. **STATUS** R.

Pied Thrush ▪ *Geokichla wardii*

DESCRIPTION Striking black-and-white thrush with conspicuous white supercilium. Female repeats pattern of male, but in her black is replaced with brown. **HABITAT** Forested areas in hills and highlands. Fond of berries of introduced Japanese Mahonia *Mahonia japonica*. Plants in *Mahonia* genus and Berberidaceae family occur naturally in its breeding grounds in the Himalayas, and may explain why it has an affinity with the berries. **DISTRIBUTION** Mid-hills to highlands. Victoria Park in Nuwara Eliya is a reliable site. **VOICE** Song described as having high-pitched notes. **STATUS** UM.

Orange-headed Thrush ▪ *Geokichla citrina citrina*

DESCRIPTION Orange head and upperparts. Wings, mantle and tail grey. In female mantle, wings and tail are browner than in male. **HABITAT** Forest patches and occasionally well-wooded gardens with plenty of leaf litter. **DISTRIBUTION** On arrival spreads from lowlands to mid-hills. **VOICE** Rich, fluty notes. **STATUS** SM.

Spot-winged Thrush ■ *Geokichla spiloptera* ⓔ

DESCRIPTION White spots on wings easy to make out. Face marked strongly with black and white. **HABITAT** Densely shaded forests. Forages for invertebrates on forest floor. **DISTRIBUTION** Wet-zone lowlands to mid-hills. Emerges to feed on trails at dawn and dusk. **VOICE** One of Sri Lanka's five species of true song bird endowed with a double larynx. Wide repertoire of call notes and rich, melodious song. **STATUS** E.

Sri Lanka Scaly Thrush ■ *Geokichla imbricata* ⓔ

DESCRIPTION Underparts brown with dark scaling unlike in Spot-winged Thrush (see above), which has white underparts with black spots. Wings do not have two white-spotted bars. Longer, heavier bill and no white spots on wings. Elusive, rarely permitting

clear view. **HABITAT** Forests from lowlands to highlands. Partial to forest patches adjoining streams. **DISTRIBUTION** Wet zone from lowlands to highlands where good-quality forest remains. Sinharaja is the best location for birders. **VOICE** Hissing call more high pitched than that of Spot-winged Thrush. Seldom sings. Song reminiscent of but different from that of Spot-winged Thrush. In March 2002 recorded singing in the evening in Horton Plains; until then it had been thought that it sang only in the mornings. **STATUS** SE. Classified as Endangered on IUCN Red List.

Indian Blackbird ■ *Turdus simillimus kinnisii*

DESCRIPTION The only all-black thrush. Beak redder than that of **Common Blackbird** *Turdus merula* found in Europe. It is possible that race *kinnisii* found in Sri Lanka may be split from race found in India. Orangish legs and reddish eye-ring. Female browner than male. **HABITAT** Bird of highlands that has adapted to human presence and visits home gardens. When 'Nillu' (*Strobilanthes* spp.) are in bloom, Horton Plains National Park seems to have a pair of Indian Blackbirds at every hundred metres. At other times these birds can be quite difficult to see in the park. **DISTRIBUTION** From mid-hills to highlands in wet zone. **VOICE** One of five songbirds resident in Sri Lanka. Beautiful and complex repertoire of rich, liquid notes. Contact calls typical thrush-like hissing notes. **STATUS** R.

Male

Sri Lanka Whistling-thrush ■ *Myophonus blighi* e

DESCRIPTION Male brownish-black with blue gloss on foreparts and blue shoulder-patch. Female brown with blue shoulder-patch. In densely shaded undergrowth favoured by these birds, they can look dull black. Whistling-thrushes are sensitive to ultraviolet light and the patterns of contrasting blue may be much more vivid to them than they appear to us. **HABITAT** Densely shaded streams. Mainly insectivorous, but opportunistically eats vertebrate animals such as geckos and agamid lizards. **DISTRIBUTION** Confined to cloud forests in central highlands and the Knuckles. Also recorded in Sinharaja East. **VOICE** Vocalizes in early morning or evening, when its shrill grating call, *sree sree, sree sree*, helps to locate it. **STATUS** SE.

LEFT: *Male*, RIGHT: *Female*

Oriental Magpie-robin ▪ *Copsychus saularis ceylonensis*

DESCRIPTION Black-and-white chat with longish tail that it raises often. Male glossy black on head, mantle and tail. In female black parts duller, almost blackish-grey. Young brown and spotted on breast. **HABITAT** Feeds primarily on the ground, although uses high perches for singing. More likely to be found in degraded habitats than in primary forest. Common garden bird. **DISTRIBUTION** Widespread from lowlands to highlands. **VOICE** Has a double larynx, making it a true songbird. Inclined to sing until late evening after light has faded. Employs a number of harsh, scolding calls. **STATUS** CR.

LEFT: *Male*, RIGHT: *Female*

White-rumped Shama
▪ *Kittacincla malabarica*

DESCRIPTION Distinctive bird with glossy blue-black upperparts, long, graduated tail, conspicuous white rump and orange-red underparts. Sexes similar, with female having slightly shorter tail than male. Occasionally perches in the open, but generally surprisingly difficult to see because it prefers to sing from within a tangled thicket, just like **Nightingale** *Luscinia megarhynchos* of Europe – another accomplished songster. This species often sings until late in the day, its song overlapping with nightjars churring at dusk. **HABITAT** Favours fairly thick lowland forests. **DISTRIBUTION** Mainly dry zone from lowlands to lower hills. **VOICE** One of the five Sri Lankan songbirds with a double larynx. Complex song of whistled notes, chattering scolding calls and mimicry vocalizations borrowed from other birds. **STATUS** R.

Indian Black Robin ■ *Saxicoloides fulicatus*

DESCRIPTION Male glossy black with white shoulder-patch and reddish-brown vent. Female brownish-black with rusty vent. **HABITAT** Lowlands and hills, forests and gardens. Occasionally a few birds take up residence in Colombo. **DISTRIBUTION** Widespread except in highlands. More common in dry lowlands. Common bird in national parks of dry lowlands. **VOICE** Repeated *chizwee* alternated with double note. Female responds to male in a lower pitch. **STATUS** R.

Female

Male

Asian Brown Flycatcher ■ *Muscicapa dauurica*

DESCRIPTION Dark legs diagnostic for separating this species from Brown-breasted Flycatcher (see p. 146), which has flesh-coloured legs. Habitat preferences also divergent. Both species have pale, dark-tipped lower mandible. Brown-breasted darker above and has browner breast-band than Asian Brown. Calls also diagnostic. **HABITAT** Bird of canopies. Occupies wooded gardens even in cities, where it can be seen flitting in search of insects. **DISTRIBUTION** Throughout Sri Lanka from lowlands to mid-hills. **VOICE** Single-noted *tchree* call. **STATUS** M.

Brown-breasted Flycatcher ▪ *Muscicapa muttui muttui*

DESCRIPTION Pale legs separate this species from Asian Brown Flycatcher (see p. 145), which has black legs. Brown-breasted also darker brown above with darker brown breast-

band. Both species have pale lower mandible. **HABITAT** Prefers wet lowland forests, but also frequents riverine vegetation in dry zone. **DISTRIBUTION** Widely distributed from lowlands to mid-hills where shaded forests are found. Absent from highlands. **VOICE** High-pitched *sree* contact call. Song very soft, as if it is singing to itself. **STATUS** M.

Dusky Blue Flycatcher ▪ *Eumyias sordidus* ℯ

DESCRIPTION Blue flycatcher with duller blue underparts fading to dirty white near vent. Loreal region black. Vocalizations, behaviour and profile different from those of energetic Black-naped Blue Monarch (see p. 117), which it is sometimes confused with. Lacks black nape. **HABITAT** Forest bird of highlands, found occasionally in mid-hills. Has adapted to human presence and also visits gardens. **DISTRIBUTION** Largely confined to highlands. Also

present in submontane areas of Eastern Sinharaja and where dry zone meets northern slopes of Knuckles Mountains. **VOICE** Light, lilting song that appears to be coming from further afield than it really is. Notes reminiscent of Indian Blackbird's song (see p. 143). **STATUS** UE. Classified as Vulnerable on IUCN Red List.

Tickell's Blue Flycatcher
▪ *Cyornis tickelliae jerdoni*

DESCRIPTION Male has blue upperparts, and black on face bordering orange throat. Orange continues to lower breast and fades into white underparts. Female lacks black on face and is duller on underparts. May be confused with vagrant **Blue-throated Flycatcher** *Cyornis rubeculoides*. Males similar but latter has blue and not orange throat. Female brown not blue on upperparts, and has whitish lores. **HABITAT** Confiding bird of forest patches throughout lowlands ascending to mid-hills. **DISTRIBUTION** Widespread from lowlands to mid-hills where shaded forests are found. Not uncommon in dry zone, but here found only in tall, shaded forests and absent from more open scrubland. **VOICE** Tinkling series of five or more notes. End of a sequence marked by a *pip-pip*. A beautiful little melody. **STATUS** R.

Male

Kashmir Flycatcher ▪ *Ficedula subrubra*

DESCRIPTION Slaty-grey upperparts. Male has black line running from bill along sides of head and bordering red throat and breast, which fades into dirty white of belly. Female lacks red on throat and breast. Both sexes have white at base of tail. Habit of raising and lowering tail. Confiding bird. **HABITAT** Mainly highlands but at times also in mid-hills. Occupies mid-storey of trees. **DISTRIBUTION** A large part of the world's Kashmir Flycatchers winter in highlands of Sri Lanka. Victoria Park in Nuwara Eliya is a well-known site. **VOICE** Contact call a rattled note. Song a whistled *chip chip* followed by a rattling note. **STATUS** SM.

Male

Indian Blue Robin ■ *Luscinia brunnea*

DESCRIPTION Male has blue upperparts, white supercilium and red underparts fading to white on vent. Facial area blackish. Female has brown upperparts; underparts lighter version of male's. **HABITAT** Hills and highlands. Skulks in dense undergrowth.

DISTRIBUTION All over Sri Lanka, except in most arid of areas and coastal regions. Number of birds increases with elevation. In hills every wooded thicket seems to have one or more of these birds, although they are very difficult to see. Victoria Park in Nuwara Eliya is top site for birders. **VOICE** Series of high-pitched *hee i* notes ending with set of 2–3 quivering notes. Once these are learnt it becomes easy to see how many individuals of this difficult-to-see bird are present in winter. **STATUS** M.

Male

Pied Bushchat ■ *Saxicola caprata atrata*

DESCRIPTION Male black and white with prominent white wing-bar, and white rump and vent. Female light brown with rusty rump. Female Indian Black Robin (see p. 145) lacks rusty rump, has longer tail and behaves more like a magpie-robin. The two species also do not share the same range. **HABITAT** Open areas interspersed with bushes and trees in highlands. **DISTRIBUTION** Grassland bordered with forest in highlands. **VOICE** Repeated, soft *chiew* contact call. Soft song of repeated, tremulous triple note a characteristic sound of highland landscape. **STATUS** UR. Classified as Endangered on IUCN Red List.

Male

Female

Golden-fronted Leafbird ■ *Chloropsis aurifrons insularis*

DESCRIPTION Male can look similar to Jerdon's Leafbird (see below), but black edge to blue throat gorget does not have diffused brownish-yellow between it and green of body. Female's forecrown yellowish and lacks male's golden colour. Juvenile all green. **HABITAT** Throughout lowlands and hills in wooded gardens and forests. **DISTRIBUTION** Widespread except in highlands. **VOICE** Complex series of notes as in Jerdon's, but plainer and less trilling. With practice the two species can be told apart by ear. **STATUS** UR. Less common than Jerdon's.

Male

Jerdon's Leafbird ■ *Chloropsis jerdoni*

DESCRIPTION Male's facial pattern similar to Golden-fronted Leafbird's (see above), but black surrounding purple centre is not as wide and extensive. Male's crown green. Female has pale blue throat faintly edged with yellow. Juveniles similar. **HABITAT** Throughout lowlands and hills in wooded gardens and forests. **DISTRIBUTION** Widespread except in highlands. **VOICE** Very complex sequence of notes often borrowing elements of calls and songs from other birds. Typically consists of whistled notes, trills and chirps. Throws in almost every type of call a passerine is capable of uttering. **STATUS** R.

Male

Thick-billed Flowerpecker ■ *Dicaeum agile zeylonicum*

DESCRIPTION Reddish irides and moustachial stripe lend this species a very different look from Pale-billed Flowerpecker (see opposite). Tail feathers tipped with white. **HABITAT** Lightly wooded areas. Visits home gardens with trees in dry lowlands. **DISTRIBUTION** North-Central, Eastern and Uva Provinces, ascending central hills on drier side. Localized in wet zone. **VOICE** Slightly tremulous, repeated *chlip chlip*. **STATUS** UR.

White-throated (Legge's) Flowerpecker ■ *Dicaeum vincens* ⓔ

DESCRIPTION White chin and throat, and yellow belly, make this species very different from the other two species of flowerpecker. Male has bluish upperparts; female duller with olive-grey upperparts. In male there is also a stronger contrast between white chin and yellow underparts. **HABITAT** Tall forests in lowlands. Habit of calling from tops of tall trees. Good views may be had when it descends low to feed on fruits such as common *Osbeckia* species along roadsides. Also takes invertebrate prey and nectar. **DISTRIBUTION** Restricted to quality forests in wet lowlands. Visits village gardens adjoining good-quality forests, but it would be misleading to think that it has adapted to forest loss. Absent where forests have been heavily fragmented. **VOICE** Males sing from high perches. Plaintive, whistled *hi-hi-hi* ascending in tone, followed by *pew-view pee-view*. **STATUS** UE. Classified as Vulnerable on IUCN Red List.

LEFT: *Male*, RIGHT: *Female*

Pale-billed Flowerpecker ■ *Dicaeum erythrorhynchos ceylonense*

DESCRIPTION Overall impression is of a small grey bird, paler below than above. Small bill distinctively downcurved. Tiniest bird in Sri Lanka. **HABITAT** Gardens and forests. **DISTRIBUTION** Throughout Sri Lanka. **VOICE** Contact call a *thlip thlip*. Song a repeated, trilling *threep*, often uttered from song perches such as TV aerials. **STATUS** CR.

Purple-rumped Sunbird ■ *Leptocoma zeylonica zeylonica*

DESCRIPTION One of Sri Lanka's smallest birds. Male absolutely stunning, with iridescent green crown, yellow belly and glistening purple rump. Female duller with brownish-grey head and dark line through eye. Both sexes constantly flick their wings. **HABITAT** Gardens and forest edges with nectar-rich plants. Mainly insectivorous but feeds opportunistically on nectar from introduced garden plants, as well as native nectaring plants. **DISTRIBUTION** Throughout Sri Lanka up to mid-hills. **VOICE** Contact call a metallic *zeut*. Song structured around core *tseep* note with various notes alternating with it. **STATUS** CR.

LEFT: *Female*, RIGHT: *Male*

Purple Sunbird ■ *Cinnyris asiaticus asiatica*

DESCRIPTION Bill shorter than in Loten's Sunbird (see below), and species use different calls. Male and female's colour patterns similar to those of Loten's. **HABITAT** Frequents home gardens but also seen in thorn-scrub forests. **DISTRIBUTION** Mainly dry lowlands. Localized in wet zone. **VOICE** Core note a metallic *cheep cheep*, rising in intonation, followed by rapidly repeated series of similar notes that end in bubbling sequence. Notes more metallic than those of Loten's. **STATUS** R.

Male

Female

Loten's Sunbird ■ *Cinnyris lotenius*

DESCRIPTION Breeding male glossy blue-black, at times iridescent green on head and mantle. Distinguishable from similar male Purple Sunbird (see above) by chocolate-brown underparts. In Purple they are glossy black. Female brownish-grey above with yellow tinged, pale underparts. Long, deeply curved bill; shorter in Purple. **HABITAT** Frequent visitor to gardens even in cities. Needs habitats where nectaring plants are easily available, and a mix of nectar and invertebrates. Young fed rich variety of invertebrates, including spiders, caterpillars and similar. **DISTRIBUTION** Most common in wet zone. **VOICE** Series of loud, metallic notes vaguely transcribing as *chewp chewp* used to announce its presence. In flight utters rapid *chik chik chik*. Sometimes utters single-noted *cheep cheep* calls. **STATUS** R.

Male

Female

Baya Weaver ▪ *Ploceus philippinus philippinus*

DESCRIPTION Can be distinguished from **Streaked Weaver** *Ploceus manyar* by lack of strong streaking on breast in both sexes of Streaked. Both sexes have pale edges to tertials. Female Streaked also has white on supercilium. Female Baya can be separated from female House Sparrow (see p. 155) by larger and stouter looking, conical bill. Female weavers darker above with heavy streaking, and lack white wing-bar found in female House Sparrow. **HABITAT** Thorn scrub bordering open clearings. At colonies their distinctive bulbous nests with entrance tunnels can be seen. **DISTRIBUTION** Throughout lowlands, but seems most prevalent in dry lowlands. **VOICE** Chittering call interspersed with wheezing notes and strong chirps. **STATUS** R.

Male

White-rumped Munia ▪ *Lonchura striata striata*

DESCRIPTION Upperparts and head dark chocolate-brown, looking black at times. Mantle feathers have thin streaks. Underparts and rump white. Bill has bluish hue. **HABITAT** Lowlands and hills. Frequents clearings and degraded forest habitats. **DISTRIBUTION** Lowlands to mid-hills. **VOICE** Usual call a twitter. Sometimes preceded by a wheezy whistle. Occasionally intersperses twitters with whistled notes. **STATUS** R.

Black-throated Munia
■ *Lonchura kelaarti*

DESCRIPTION Black throat and face, and scaly underneath like Scaly-breasted Munia (see below), but much darker on upperparts. May visit degraded sites such as the Elephant Nook wetland in Nuwara Eliya, and confusion is possible with more common Scaly-breasted. **HABITAT** Mainly highland forests with open areas. Occasionally lower hills. **DISTRIBUTION** Mainly highlands but occasionally seen in wet lowlands, for example in Sinharaja. May employ seasonal movements in search of food. **VOICE** Nasal, repeated *cheep cheep*. Quite distinct from calls of other munias. **STATUS** UR. Classified as Vulnerable on IUCN Red List.

Scaly-breasted Munia ■ *Lonchura punctulata punctulata*

DESCRIPTION Brown head and upperparts; brown on throat up to breast. Underparts white with neat black scales. Vocalizes a lot, which helps to avoid confusion with rarer

Black-throated Munia (see above) where their ranges overlap. **HABITAT** Degraded forest habitats in lowlands, grassland and disturbed habitats with colonizing tall grass. **DISTRIBUTION** Throughout Sri Lanka. Found in large numbers in dry lowlands and considered a pest by farmers. **VOICE** Distinct, clear *pit-teuw*; more of a whistled tone than nasal chirp characteristic of most munias. **STATUS** R.

Tri-coloured Munia ■ *Lonchura malacca*

DESCRIPTION Black head, chestnut upperparts and white breast bordered around vent in black. Heavy silvery bill. Juveniles plainer than those of Scaly-breasted Munia (see opposite) and also told apart by heavy silvery bill. **HABITAT** Grassland. **DISTRIBUTION** Throughout Sri Lanka. Birds probably travel a lot in search of food, as small flocks can turn up even in small plots of wasteland in cities. **VOICE** Series of repeated, nasal chirps. **STATUS** R.

House Sparrow

■ *Passer domesticus indicus*

DESCRIPTION Male has grey crown and is more richly coloured than female. Fresh feathers on male wear off to reveal black bib during breeding season. **HABITAT** Village-garden habitats, which are edge habitats, with access to grain. **DISTRIBUTION** Throughout Sri Lanka. Numbers have declined; a phenomenon observed worldwide. A few decades ago, rice was sieved in flat wicker trays to separate the chaff and stones, which were cast aside on the ground. Earthen pots were hung as nest boxes for House Sparrows, so the birds had both food and nest sites. The change to the use of supermarket ready-cleaned grain may be one of many factors accounting for the demise of House Sparrows in cities. **VOICE** Series of repeated chirps. Also *cheep-cheep-churp-churp.* **STATUS** R.

Forest Wagtail
■ *Dendronanthus indicus*

DESCRIPTION Unlikely to be confused with any other wagtail, with its boldly white-barred, blackish wings, brown mantle and crown, and white underparts. Two broad black bands on breast in both sexes, which cannot be told apart. **HABITAT** Forest patches or large home gardens. Forages in leaf litter in densely shaded thickets. **DISTRIBUTION** On arrival spreads throughout Sri Lanka. **VOICE** Characteristic *plink plink* call that betrays its presence. **STATUS** M.

Western Yellow Wagtail ■ *Motacilla flava*

DESCRIPTION Advanced field guides may need to be consulted to distinguish the several races that occur (or potentially occur) in Sri Lanka. Adults in non-breeding plumage and immatures can present significant identification challenges. By and large, most of the yellow wagtails seen are likely to be of race M. *f. thunbergi*, or Grey-headed Yellow Wagtail. **HABITAT** Wet habitats in lowlands. Lake edges, marshes, ploughed paddy fields and similar. **DISTRIBUTION** Spreads throughout Sri Lanka on arrival. **VOICE** High-pitched *shree shree* double-noted call. Very different from Grey Wagtail's (see opposite) single, repeated note. **STATUS** Race *thunbergi* a regular migrant in small numbers; other migrant races rare.

Winter

Grey Wagtail ■ *Motacilla cinerea melanope*

DESCRIPTION Grey crown and mantle, white supercilium and yellow underparts with some white on flanks. Non-breeding adult has white throat. Breeding adult has black chin and throat, and white malar stripe. Most birds seen in Sri Lanka are in non-breeding plumage. **HABITAT** Favours banks and grassy areas adjacent to water. **DISTRIBUTION** Spreads throughout Sri Lanka on arrival. Appears to prefer higher elevations and likelihood of encountering it increases with elevation. **VOICE** Clearly articulated *tchink tchink* uttered in quick succession and repeated. **STATUS** M.

Winter

Richard's Pipit ■ *Anthus richardi richardi*

DESCRIPTION Pale lores (can look dark at times); usually has an upright stance and gives an impression of having to drag a heavy tail. Long hind claw. Larger than Paddyfield Pipit (see p. 158) but this may not be apparent unless a comparison is possible. **HABITAT** Short grassland and open areas in dry lowlands. **DISTRIBUTION** Seems most abundant in northern parts of Sri Lanka. **VOICE** Distinct, repeated *cheep*. Quite different from call of Paddyfield. **STATUS** SM.

Paddyfield Pipit ▪ *Anthus rufulus malayensis*

DESCRIPTION Common pipit, although unfortunately there is no clear feature identifying a bird as a Paddyfield Pipit and the identification is relative. Confusion most

likely with scarce migrant Richard's Pipit (see p. 157). Like Richard's this species has tawny flanks and long hind-claws, but bill is finer. Longer hind-claw in Richard's not always apparent in the field. Calls are the most reliable features for distinguishing the species. Paddyfield can look 'different' due to age, moult or lighting conditions. At times it can raise feathers on its crown; it has a distinct supercilium and malar stripe, and rusty cheek-coverts. These features are, however, also shared with other pipits. **HABITAT** Areas of short grass. **DISTRIBUTION** Widespread from lowlands to highlands. **VOICE** Call sequence is *chip chip chip-chip-chip*. **STATUS** R.

Blyth's Pipit ▪ *Anthus godlewskii*

DESCRIPTION 'Blunt-tipped' median coverts and call are the key diagnostics. Streaked bands on upper breast seem finer and tidier compared with Paddyfield Pipit's (see above).

Blyth's, Paddyfield and Richard's Pipits all have unstreaked bellies. Compared with Richard's, bill of this species is finer. **HABITAT** Grassy pastures in dry lowlands. **DISTRIBUTION** Recorded mainly from Uda Walawe National Park, where it is a recurrent visitor. **VOICE** Repeated, nasal, single-noted *chew*. **STATUS** SM.

For an explanation of the status acronyms, see the introduction (p. 16). Some species have two or more subspecies (races) recorded in Sri Lanka, in which the status is given for each species. For simplicity, in this checklist species are shown only at species level, ignoring the trinomials for the subspecies level. In the main body of the text, trinomials (based on Wijesinghe, 1994) are provided in some of the species accounts.

In this checklist, the common and scientific names have been revised to largely follow the nomenclature and taxonomy in the *HBW and Birdlife International Illustrated Checklist of the Birds of the World* (de Hoyo & Collar, 2014). However, key departures at species level are Steppe Gull *Larus [cachinnans] barabensis*, Sri Lanka Scaly Thrush *Geokichla imbricata*, Eastern (Siberian) Stonechat *Saxicola maurus*, 'Desert' Whitethroat *Sylvia [curruca] minula* and Hume's Whitethroat *Sylvia althaea* (the last two considered subspecies of Lesser Whitethroat *Sylvia curruca*). These are retained at species or putative species level. This is to draw attention to subspecies that are recognized as full species by some authors.

	Order GALLIFORMES	
	Phasianidae (Partridges, Quails and Pheasants)	
1	Indian Peafowl *Pavo cristatus*	R
2	Rain Quail *Coturnix coromandelica*	HSM
3	Asian Blue Quail *Coturnix chinensis*	SR
4	Jungle Bush-quail *Perdicula asiatica*	SR
5	Painted Francolin *Francolinus pictus*	SR
6	Grey Francolin *Francolinus pondicerianus*	UR
7	Sri Lanka Spurfowl *Galloperdix bicalcarata*	UE
8	Sri Lanka Junglefowl *Gallus lafayetii*	CE
	Order ANSERIFORMES	
	Anatidae (Swans, Geese and Ducks)	
9	Fulvous Whistling-duck *Dendrocygna bicolor*	V, R
10	Lesser Whistling-duck *Dendrocygna javanica*	R
11	Greylag Goose *Anser anser*	V
12	Bar-headed Goose *Anser indicus*	V
13	Ruddy Shelduck *Tadorna ferruginea*	V
14	African Comb Duck *Sarkidiornis melanotos*	HSM
15	Cotton Pygmy-goose *Nettapus coromandelianus*	UR
16	Ferruginous Duck *Aythya nyroca*	V
17	Tufted Duck *Aythya fuligula*	V
18	Gadwall *Mareca strepera*	V
19	Eurasian Wigeon *Mareca penelope*	M
20	Indian Spot-billed Duck *Anas poecilorhyncha*	HSR, SM
21	Common Teal *Anas crecca*	SM
22	Northern Pintail *Anas acuta*	M
23	Garganey *Spatula querquedula*	M
24	Northern Shoveler *Spatula clypeata*	SM
	Order PODICIPEDIFORMES	
	Podicipedidae (Grebes)	
25	Little Grebe *Tachybaptus ruficollis*	R

Order PHOENICOPTERIFORMES

Phoenicopteridae (Flamingos)

26	Greater Flamingo *Phoenicopterus roseus*	M
27	Lesser Flamingo *Phoeniconaias minor*	V

Order PHAETHONTIFORMES

Phaethontidae (Tropicbirds)

28	White-tailed Tropicbird *Phaethon lepturus*	SM
29	Red-billed Tropicbird *Phaethon aethereus*	SM

Order COLUMBIFORMES

Columbidae (Pigeons and Doves)

30	Rock Pigeon *Columba livia*	UR
31	Sri Lanka Woodpigeon *Columba torringtoniae*	UE
32	Pale-capped Pigeon *Columba punicea*	V
33	Oriental Turtle-dove *Streptopelia orientalis*	HSM
34	Western Spotted Dove *Spilopelia suratensis*	CR
35	Red Turtle-dove *Streptopelia tranquebarica*	V
36	Eurasian Collared-dove *Streptopelia decaocto*	UR
37	Grey-capped Emerald Dove *Chalcophaps indica*	R
38	Orange-breasted Green-pigeon *Treron bicinctus*	R
39	Sri Lanka Green-pigeon *Treron pompadora*	E
40	Yellow-footed Green-pigeon *Treron phoenicopterus*	HSM, HSR
41	Green Imperial-pigeon *Ducula aenea*	R

Order CAPRIMULGIFORMES

Podargidae (Frogmouths)

42	Ceylon Frogmouth *Batrachostomus moniliger*	R

Caprimulgidae (Nightjars)

43	Great Eared-nightjar *Eurostopodus macrotis*	V
44	Jungle Nightjar *Caprimulgus indicus*	UR
45	Jerdon's Nightjar *Caprimulgus atripennis*	R
46	Indian Little Nightjar *Caprimulgus asiaticus*	R

Hemiprocnidae (Treeswifts)

47	Crested Treeswift *Hemiprocne coronata*	R

Apodidae (Swifts)

48	Indian Swiftlet *Aerodramus unicolor*	R
49	Himalayan Swiftlet *Aerodramus brevirostris*	V
50	Brown-throated Needletail *Hirundapus giganteus*	SR
51	Asian Palm-swift *Cypsiurus balasiensis*	R
52	Alpine Swift *Tachymarptis melba*	UR
53	Pacific Swift *Apus pacificus*	V
54	Little Swift *Apus affinis*	R

Order CUCULIFORMES

Cuculidae (Cuckoos)

55	Green-billed Coucal *Centropus chlororhynchos*	HSE
56	Greater Coucal *Centropus parroti*	CR
57	Sirkeer Malkoha *Taccocua leschenaultii*	UR
58	Red-faced Malkoha *Phaenicophaeus pyrrhocephalus*	SE
59	Blue-faced Malkoha *Phaenicophaeus viridirostris*	UR
60	Chestnut-winged Cuckoo *Clamator coromandu*	UM

61	Jacobin Cuckoo *Clamator jacobinus*	UR
62	Western Koel *Eudynamys scolopaceus*	CR
63	Asian Emerald Cuckoo *Chrysococcyx maculatus*	V
64	Banded Bay Cuckoo *Cacomantis sonneratii*	UR
65	Grey-bellied Cuckoo *Cacomantis passerinus*	M
66	Fork-tailed Drongo-cuckoo *Surniculus [lugubris] dicruroides*	UR
67	Common Hawk-cuckoo *Hierococcyx varius*	UR, HSM
68	Small Cuckoo *Cuculus poliocephalus*	SM
69	Indian Cuckoo *Cuculus micropterus*	UR, M
70	Common Cuckoo *Cuculus canorus*	SM

Order GRUIFORMES
Rallidae (Rails, Crakes, Gallinules and Coots)

71	Slaty-legged Crake *Rallina eurizonoides*	UM, HSR
72	Indian Water Rail *Rallus indicus*	V
73	Slaty-breasted Rail *Lewinia striatus*	UR, UM
74	Corn Crake *Crex crex*	V
75	White-breasted Waterhen *Amaurornis phoenicurus*	CR
76	Baillon's Crake *Zapornia pusilla*	HSM
77	Ruddy-breasted Crake *Porzana fusca*	UR
78	Watercock *Gallicrex cinerea*	UR
79	Purple Swamphen *Porphyrio poliocephalus*	R
80	Common Moorhen *Gallinula chloropus*	R
81	Eurasian Coot *Fulica atra*	UR,SM

Order PROCELLARIIFORMES
Oceanitidae (Southern Storm-Petrels)

82	Wilson's Storm-Petrel *Oceanites oceanicus*	M
83	White-faced Storm-Petrel *Pelagodroma marina*	V
84	Black-bellied Storm-Petrel *Fregetta tropica*	V

Hydrobatidae (Northern Storm-Petrels)

85	Swinhoe's Storm-Petrel *Hydrobates monorhis*	SM

Procellariidae (Petrels and Shearwaters)

86	Cape Petrel *Daption capense*	V
87	Barau's Petrel *Pterodroma baraui*	HSM
88	Bulwer's Petrel *Bulweria bulwerii*	V
89	Jouanin's Petrel *Bulweria fallax*	V
90	Streaked Shearwater *Calonectris leucomelas*	V
91	Wedge-tailed Shearwater *Ardenna pacifica*	M
92	Sooty Shearwater *Ardenna griseus*	V
93	Flesh-footed Shearwater *Ardenna carneipes*	M
94	Short-tailed Shearwater *Ardenna tenuirostris*	V
95	Persian Shearwater *Puffinus persicus*	SM

Order CICONIIFORMES
Ciconiidae (Storks)

96	Painted Stork *Mycteria leucocephala*	R
97	Asian Openbill *Anastomus oscitans*	R
98	Black Stork *Ciconia nigra*	V
99	Woolly-necked Stork *Ciconia episcopus*	UR
100	White Stork *Ciconia ciconia*	V

101	Black-necked Stork *Ephippiorhynchus asiaticus*	HSR
102	Lesser Adjutant *Leptoptilos javanicus*	SR

Order PELICANIFORMES

Threskiornithidae (Ibises and Spoonbills)

103	Glossy Ibis *Plegadis falcinellus*	SM
104	Black-headed Ibis *Threskiornis melanocephalus*	R
105	Eurasian Spoonbill *Platalea leucorodia*	UR

Ardeidae (Herons and Egrets)

106	Little Egret *Egretta garzetta*	CR
107	Western Reef-egret *Egretta gularis*	SM
108	Great Egret *Ardea alba*	CR
109	Intermediate Egret *Ardea intermedia*	CR
110	Grey Heron *Ardea cinerea*	R
111	Goliath Heron *Ardea goliath*	V
112	Purple Heron *Ardea purpurea*	R
113	Cattle Egret *Bubulcus ibis*	CR
114	Indian Pond Heron *Ardeola grayii*	CR
115	Chinese Pond Heron *Ardeola bacchus*	V
116	Striated Heron *Butorides striata*	UR
117	Black-crowned Night-heron *Nycticorax nycticorax*	UR
118	Malayan Night-heron *Gorsachius melanolophus*	SM
119	Yellow Bittern *Ixobrychus sinensis*	UR, M
120	Chestnut Bittern *Ixobrychus cinnamomeus*	UR
121	Schrenk's Bittern *Ixobrychus eurhythmus*	V
122	Black Bittern *Ixobrychus flavicollis*	UR, M
123	Eurasian Bittern *Botaurus stellaris*	V

Pelecanidae (Pelicans)

124	Spot-billed Pelican *Pelecanus philippensis*	R

Order SULIFORMES

Fregatidae (Frigatebirds)

125	Lesser Frigatebird *Fregata ariel*	HSM
126	Great Frigatebird *Fregata minor*	HSM
127	Christmas Frigatebird *Fregata andrewsi*	HSM

Sulidae (Gannets and Boobies)

128	Masked Booby *Sula dactylatra*	SM
129	Brown Booby *Sula leucogaster*	SM
130	Red-footed Booby *Sula sula*	V

Phalacrocoracidae (Cormorants and Shags)

131	Little Cormorant *Microcarbo niger*	CR
132	Indian Shag *Phalacrocorax fuscicollis*	CR
133	Great Cormorant *Phalacrocorax carbo*	SR

Anhingidae (Darters)

134	Oriental Darter *Anhinga melanogaster*	UR

Order CHARADRIIFORMES

Burhinidae (Thick-knees)

135	Indian Thick-knee (Stone-curlew) *Burhinus indicus*	SR
136	Great Thick-knee *Esacus recurvirostris*	UR

Haematopodidae (Oystercatchers)

137	Eurasian Oystercatcher *Haematopus ostralegus*	SM
Recurvirostridae (Avocets and Stilts)		
138	Pied Avocet *Recurvirostra avosetta*	SM
139	Black-winged Stilt *Himantopus himantopus*	CR, M
Charadriidae (Plovers)		
140	Pacific Golden Plover *Pluvialis fulva*	M
141	Grey Plover *Pluvialis squatarola*	UM
142	Common Ringed Plover *Charadrius hiaticula*	SM
143	Little Ringed Plover *Charadrius dubius*	UR, UM
144	Kentish Plover *Charadrius alexandrinus*	UR, UM
145	Lesser Sand Plover *Charadrius mongolus*	M
146	Greater Sand Plover *Charadrius leschenaultii*	SM
147	Caspian Plover *Charadrius asiaticus*	SM
148	Oriental Plover *Charadrius veredus*	V
149	Yellow-wattled Lapwing *Vanellus malarbaricus*	UR
150	Grey headed Lapwing *Vanellus cinereus*	V
151	Red-wattled Lapwing *Vanellus indicus*	CR
152	Sociable Plover *Vanellus gregarius*	V
Rostratulidae (Painted-snipes)		
153	Greater Painted-snipe *Rostratula benghalensis*	UR
Jacanidae (Jacanas)		
154	Pheasant-tailed Jacana *Hydrophasianus chirurgus*	R
Scolopacidae (Sandpipers and allies)		
155	Whimbrel *Numenius phaeopus*	UM
156	Eurasian Curlew *Numenius arquata*	UM
157	Black-tailed Godwit *Limosa limosa*	M, HSM
158	Bar-tailed Godwit *Limosa lapponica*	SM
159	Ruddy Turnstone *Arenaria interpres*	M
160	Great Knot *Calidris tenuirostris*	HSM
161	Red Knot *Calidris canutus*	V
162	Sanderling *Calidris alba*	UM
163	Little Stint *Calidris minuta*	CM
164	Red-necked Stint *Calidris ruficollis*	V
165	Temminck's Stint *Calidris temminckii*	SM
166	Long-toed Stint *Calidris subminuta*	SM
167	Sharp-tailed Sandpiper *Calidris acuminata*	V
168	Pectoral Sandpiper *Calidris melanotos*	V
169	Dunlin *Calidris alpina*	V
170	Curlew Sandpiper *Calidris ferruginea*	CM
171	Spoon-billed Sandpiper *Calidris pygmeus*	V
172	Buff-breasted Sandpiper *Calidris subruficollis*	V
173	Broad-billed Sandpiper *Calidris falcinellus*	UM
174	Ruff *Calidris pugnax*	UM
175	Asian Dowitcher *Limnodromus semipalmatus*	V
176	Eurasian Woodcock *Scolopax rusticola*	HSM
177	Wood Snipe *Gallinago nemoricola*	V
178	Pintail Snipe *Gallinago stenura*	M

179	Swinhoe's Snipe *Gallinago megala*	V
180	Common Snipe *Gallinago gallinago*	UM
181	Great Snipe *Gallinago media*	V
182	Jack Snipe *Lymnocryptes minimus*	HSM
183	Red-necked Phalarope *Phalaropus lobatus*	SM
184	Spotted Redshank *Tringa erythropus*	V
185	Common Redshank *Tringa totanus*	CM
186	Common Greenshank *Tringa nebularia*	UM
187	Marsh Sandpiper *Tringa stagnatilis*	CM
188	Green Sandpiper *Tringa ochropus*	UM
189	Wood Sandpiper *Tringa glareola*	M
190	Terek Sandpiper *Xenus cinereus*	UM
191	Common Sandpiper *Actitis hypoleucos*	M
Turnicidae (Buttonquails)		
192	Barred Buttonquail *Turnix suscitator*	R
193	Small Buttonquail *Turnix sylvaticus*	V
Dromadidae (Crab-plovers)		
194	Crab-plover *Dromas ardeola*	SR
Glareolidae (Coursers and Pratincoles)		
195	Indian Courser *Cursorius coromandelicus*	HSR
196	Collared Pratincole *Glareola pratincola*	SM
197	Oriental Pratincole *Glareola maldivarum*	UR
198	Small Pratincole *Glareola lactea*	UR
Laridae (Gulls, Terns and Skimmers)		
199	Brown Noddy *Anous stolidus*	UM, HSR
200	Lesser Noddy *Anous tenuirostris*	HSM
201	Sooty Gull *Larus hemprichii*	V
202	Lesser Black-backed Gull (ssp. Heuglin's Gull) *Larus fuscus*	M
203	Steppe Gull *Larus [cachinnans] barabensis*	V
204	Pallas's or Great Black-headed Gull *Larus ichthyaetus*	M
205	Brown-headed Gull *Larus brunnicephalus*	M
206	Black-headed Gull *Larus ridibundus*	SM
207	Slender-billed Gull *Larus genei*	V
208	Gull-billed Tern *Gelochelidon nilotica*	SR, CM
209	Caspian Tern *Hydroprogne caspia*	SR, M
210	Lesser Crested Tern *Thalasseus bengalensis*	M
211	Great Crested Tern *Thalasseus bergii*	R, V
212	Sandwich Tern *Thalasseus sandvicensis*	HSM
213	Roseate Tern *Sterna dougallii*	UR
214	Black-naped Tern *Sterna sumatrana*	V
215	Common Tern *Sterna hirundo*	SR, SM, M
216	Little Tern *Sternula albifrons*	R
217	White-cheeked Tern *Sterna repressa*	V
218	Saunders's Tern *Sternula saundersi*	HSR
219	Bridled or Brown-winged Tern *Onychoprion anaethetus*	M, HSR
220	Sooty Tern *Onychoprion fuscatus*	SM, HSR
221	Whiskered Tern *Chlidonias hybrida*	CM
222	White-winged Tern *Chlidonias leucopterus*	M

	Stercorariidae (Skuas)	
223	Brown Skua *Catharacta antarctica*	SM
224	South Polar Skua *Catharacta maccormicki*	V
225	Pomarine Skua *Stercorarius pomarinus*	M
226	Parasitic Skua *Stercorarius parasiticus*	HSM
227	Long-tailed Skua *Stercorarius longicaudus*	V

Order STRIGIFORMES

	Tytonidae (Barn-owls)	
228	Ceylon Bay Owl *Phodilus assimilis*	HSR
229	Common Barn-owl *Tyto alba*	SR

	Strigidae (Typical owls)	
230	Brown Boobook *Ninox scutulata*	R
231	Short-eared Owl *Asio flammeus*	SM
232	Jungle Owlet *Glaucidium radiatum*	R
233	Chestnut-backed Owlet *Glaucidium castanotum*	E
234	Serendib Scops-owl *Otus thilohoffmanni*	SE
235	Oriental Scops-owl *Otus sunia*	SR
236	Indian Scops-owl *Otus bakkamoena*	R
237	Spot-bellied Eagle-owl *Bubo nipalensis*	UR
238	Brown Fish-owl *Ketupa zeylonensis*	R
239	Brown Wood-owl *Strix leptogrammica*	UR

Order ACCIPITRIFORMES

	Pandionidae (Ospreys)	
240	Osprey *Pandion haliaetus*	SM

	Accipitridae (Hawks, Kites, Eagles and Vultures)	
241	Black-winged Kite *Elanus caeruleus*	UR
242	Jerdon's Baza *Aviceda jerdoni*	SR
243	Black Baza *Aviceda leuphotes*	V
244	Oriental Honey-buzzard *Pernis ptilorhyncus*	UR, SM
245	European Honey-buzzard *Pernis apivorus*	V
246	Egyptian Vulture *Neophron percnopterus*	V
247	Crested Serpent-eagle *Spilornis cheela*	R
248	Black Kite *Milvus migrans*	SR, M
249	Brahminy Kite *Haliastur indus*	R
250	White-bellied Sea-eagle *Haliaeetus leucogaster*	UR
251	Grey-headed Fish-eagle *Ichthyophaga ichthyaetus*	SR
252	Western Marsh Harrier *Circus aeruginosus*	UM
253	Pallid Harrier *Circus macrourus*	UM
254	Pied Harrier *Circus melanoleucos*	V
255	Montagu's Harrier *Circus pygargus*	UM
256	Crested Goshawk *Accipiter trivirgatus*	UR
257	Shikra *Accipiter badius*	R
258	Besra Sparrowhawk *Accipiter virgatus*	SR
259	Eurasian Sparrowhawk *Accipiter nisus*	V
260	Eurasian Buzzard *Buteo buteo*	SM
261	Long-legged Buzzard *Buteo rufinus*	HSM
262	Black Eagle *Ictinaetus malaiensis*	UR
263	Tawny Eagle *Aquila rapax*	V

264	Bonelli's Eagle *Aquila fasciatus*	V
265	Greater Spotted Eagle *Clanga clanga*	V
266	Booted Eagle *Hieraaetus pennatus*	SM
267	Rufous-bellied Eagle *Lophotriorchis kienerii*	UR
268	Crested Hawk-eagle *Nisaetus cirrhatus*	R
269	Mountain or Legge's Hawk-eagle *Nisaetus nipalensis*	SR

Order TROGONIFORMES

Trogonidae (Trogons)

| 270 | Malabar Trogon *Harpactes fasciatus* | UR |

Order BUCEROTIFORMES

Bucerotidae (Hornbills)

| 271 | Sri Lanka Grey Hornbill *Ocyceros gingalensis* | E |
| 272 | Malabar Pied Hornbill *Anthracoceros coronatus* | R |

Upupidae (Hoopoes)

| 273 | Common Hoopoe *Upupa epops* | UR |

Order CORACIIFORMES

Meropidae (Bee-eaters)

274	Asian or Little Green Bee-eater *Merops orientalis*	R
275	Blue-tailed Bee-eater *Merops philippinus*	CM
276	European Bee-eater *Merops apiaster*	SM
277	Chestnut-headed Bee-eater *Merops leschenaulti*	UR

Coraciidae (Rollers)

278	Indian Roller *Coracias benghalensis*	R
279	European Roller *Coracias garrulus*	V
280	Dollarbird *Eurystomus orientalis*	HSR

Alcedinidae (Kingfishers)

281	Common Kingfisher *Alcedo atthis*	R
282	Blue-eared Kingfisher *Alcedo meninting*	HSR
283	Black-backed Dwarf Kingfisher *Ceyx erithaca*	UR
284	Pied Kingfisher *Ceryle rudis*	UR
285	Stork-billed Kingfisher *Pelargopsis capensis*	UR
286	White-throated Kingfisher *Halcyon smyrnensis*	CR
287	Black-capped Kingfisher *Halcyon pileata*	SM

Order PICIFORMES

Megalamidae (Barbets)

288	Brown-headed Barbet *Psilopogon zeylanica*	CR
289	Yellow-fronted Barbet *Psilopogon flavifrons*	E
290	Sri Lanka Small Barbet *Psilopogon rubricapillus*	CE
291	Coppersmith Barbet *Psilopogon haemacephala*	R

Picidae (Woodpeckers)

292	Eurasian Wryneck *Jynx torquilla*	HSM
293	Greater Sri Lanka Flameback *Chrysocolaptes stricklandi*	E
294	White-naped Flameback *Chrysocolaptes festivus*	SR
295	Indian or Brown-capped Pygmy Woodpecker *Dendrocopos nanus*	UR
296	Yellow-crowned Woodpecker *Dendrocopos mahrattensis*	UR
297	Rufous Woodpecker *Micropternus brachyurus*	UR
298	Lesser Yellownape *Picus chlorolophus*	R
299	Streak-throated Woodpecker *Picus xanthopygaeus*	SR

300	Black-rumped (Golden-backed) Woodpecker *Dinopium benghalense*	UR
301	Lesser Sri Lanka Flameback *Dinopium psarodes*	CE

Order FALCONIFORMES

Falconidae (Falcons)

302	Lesser Kestrel *Falco naumanni*	V
303	Common Kestrel *Falco tinnunculus*	HSR, UM, HSM
304	Red-headed Falcon *Falco chicquera*	V
305	Amur Falcon *Falco amurensis*	HSM
306	Eurasian Hobby *Falco subbuteo*	V
307	Oriental Hobby *Falco severus*	V
308	Peregrine Falcon *Falco peregrinus*	UR,SM

Order PSITTACIFORMES

Psittacidae (Parrots)

309	Sri Lanka Hanging-parrot *Loriculus beryllinus*	CE
310	Alexandrine Parakeet *Psittacula eupatria*	R
311	Rose-ringed Parakeet *Psittacula krameri*	CR
312	Plum-headed Parakeet *Psittacula cyanocephala*	UR
313	Emerald Collared or Layard's Parakeet *Psittacula calthropae*	UE

Order PASSERIFORMES

Pittidae (Pittas)

314	Indian Pitta *Pitta brachyura*	M

Oriolidae (Old World Orioles)

315	Eurasian Golden Oriole *Oriolus oriolus*	SM
316	Indian Golden Oriole *Oriolus kundoo*	SM
317	Black-naped Oriole *Oriolus chinensis*	V
318	Black-hooded Oriole *Oriolus xanthornus*	R

Campephagidae (Cuckooshrikes)

319	Small Minivet *Pericrocotus cinnamomeus*	R
320	Scarlet Minivet *Pericrocotus flammeus*	R
321	Indian or Large Cuckooshrike *Coracina macei*	UR
322	Black-headed Cuckooshrike *Lalage melanoptera*	R

Artamidae (Woodswallows)

323	Ashy Woodswallow *Artamus fuscus*	UR

Vangidae (Vangas and allies)

324	Pied Flycatcher-shrike *Hemipus picatus*	UR
325	Sri Lanka Woodshrike *Tephrodornis affinis*	E

Aegithinidae (Ioras)

326	Common Iora *Aegithina tiphia*	R
327	Marshall's Iora *Aegithina nigrolutea*	SR

Rhipiduridae (Fantails)

328	White-browed Fantail *Rhipidura aureola*	R

Cicruridae (Drongos)

329	Black Drongo *Dicrurus macrocercus*	UR
330	Ashy Drongo *Dicrurus leucophaeus*	UM
331	White-bellied Drongo *Dicrurus caerulescens*	CR
332	Greater Racket-tailed Drongo *Dicrurus paradiseus*	UR
333	Sri Lanka Crested Drongo *Dicrurus lophorinus*	UE

Monarchidae (Monarch Flycatchers)		
334	Indian Paradise Flycatcher *Terpsiphone paradisi*	R, M
335	Black-naped Blue Monarch *Hypothymis azurea*	UR
Laniidae (Shrikes)		
336	Brown Shrike *Lanius cristatus*	CM, SM
337	Bay-backed Shrike *Lanius vittatus*	V
338	Long-tailed Shrike *Lanius schach*	SR
339	Great Grey Shrike *Lanius excubitor*	V
Corvidae (Crows and Jays)		
340	Sri Lanka Blue Magpie *Urocissa ornata*	UE
341	House Crow *Corvus splendens*	CR
342	Indian Jungle Crow *Corvus macrorhynchos*	R
Hyliotidae (Hyliotas)		
343	Grey-headed Canary-flycatcher *Culicicapa ceylonensis*	UR
Paridae (Tits)		
344	Great Tit *Parus major*	R
Alaudidae (Larks)		
345	Jerdon's Bushlark *Mirafra affinis*	R
346	Ashy-crowned Sparrow-lark *Eremopterix griseus*	UR
347	Greater Short-toed Lark *Calandrella brachydactyla*	V
348	Oriental Skylark *Alauda gulgula*	UR, SR
Cisticolidae (Cisticolas and allies)		
349	Zitting Cisticola *Cisticola juncidis*	R
350	Grey-breasted Prinia *Prinia hodgsonii*	UR
351	Ashy Prinia *Prinia socialis*	R
352	Jungle Prinia *Prinia sylvatica*	R
353	Plain Prinia *Prinia inornata*	R
354	Common Tailorbird *Orthotomus sutorius*	CR
Acrocephalidae (Reed-warblers)		
355	Blyth's Reed-warbler *Acrocephalus dumetorum*	CM
356	Black-browed Reed-warbler *Acrocephalus bistrigiceps*	V
357	Indian Reed-warbler *Acrocephalus stentoreus*	UR
358	Sykes's Warbler *Iduna rama*	SM
359	Booted Warbler *Iduna caligata*	V
Locustellidae (Grasshopper-warblers and Grassbirds)		
360	Lanceolated Warbler *Locustella lanceolata*	V
361	Common Grasshopper Warbler *Locustella naevia*	V
362	Rusty-rumped Warbler *Locustella certhiola*	SM
363	Sri Lanka Bush-warbler *Elaphrornis palliseri*	UE
364	Indian Broad-tailed Grass-warbler *Schoenicola platyurus*	V
Hirundinidae (Swallows and Martins)		
365	Collared Sand-martin *Riparia riparia*	SM
366	Dusky Crag-martin *Ptyonoprogne concolor*	V
367	Barn Swallow *Hirundo rustica*	CM, UM, SM
368	House or Hill Swallow *Hirundo javanica*	R
369	Wire-tailed Swallow *Hirundo smithii*	V
370	Red-rumped Swallow *Hirundo daurica*	SM, HSM
371	Sri Lanka Swallow *Cecropsis hyperythra*	E

372	Streak-throated Swallow *Petrochelidon fluvicola*	V
373	Northern House-martin *Delichon urbicum*	V

Pycnonotidae (Bulbuls)

374	Black-capped Bulbul *Pycnonotus melanicterus*	UE
375	Red-vented Bulbul *Pycnonotus cafer*	CR
376	Yellow-eared Bulbul *Pycnonotus penicillatus*	E
377	White-browed Bulbul *Pycnonotus luteolus*	R
378	Yellow-browed Bulbul *Acritillas indica*	UR
379	Square-tailed Black Bulbul *Hypsipetes ganeesa*	UR

Phylloscopidae (Leaf-warblers)

380	Dusky Warbler *Phylloscopus fuscatus*	V
381	Greenish Warbler *Phylloscopus trochiloides*	SM
382	Green or Bright-green Warbler *Phylloscopus nitidus*	CM
383	Large-billed Leaf-warbler *Phylloscopus magnirostris*	CM
384	Western Crowned Warbler *Phylloscopus occipitalis*	V

Sylviidae (Old World Warblers)

385	Lesser Whitethroat *Sylvia curruca*	V
386	Desert' Whitethroat *Sylvia [curruca] minula*	V
387	Hume's Whitethroat *Sylvia althaea*	SM

Zosteropidae (White-eyes)

388	Sri Lanka White-eye *Zosterops ceylonensis*	E
389	Oriental White-eye *Zosterops palpebrosus*	R

Timaliidae (Scimitar-babblers and allies)

390	Ashy-headed Laughingthrush *Garrulax cinereifrons*	SE
391	Sri Lanka Scimitar-babbler *Pomatorhinus melanurus*	UE
392	Tawny-bellied Babbler *Dumetia hyperythra*	UR
393	Dark-fronted Babbler *Rhopocichla atriceps*	R
394	Yellow-eyed Babbler *Chrysomma sinense*	R
395	Orange-billed or Sri Lanka Rufous Babbler *Turdoides rufescens*	UE
396	Yellow-billed Babbler *Turdoides affinis*	CR

Pellorneidae (Ground Babblers)

397	Brown-capped Babbler *Pellorneum fuscocapillus*	UE

Sittidae (Nuthatches)

398	Velvet-fronted Nuthatch *Sitta frontalis*	R

Sturnidae (Starlings)

399	White-faced Starling *Sturnornis albofrontatus*	HSE
400	Chestnut-tailed or Grey-headed Starling *Sturnia malabarica*	V
401	Daurian Starling *Agropsar sturninus*	V
402	Brahminy Starling *Sturnia pagodarum*	M
403	Rosy Starling *Pastor roseus*	M
404	Common Starling *Sturnus vulgaris*	V
405	Common Myna *Acridotheres tristis*	CR
406	Sri Lanka Hill-myna *Gracula ptilogenys*	UE
407	Southern Hill-myna *Gracula indica*	R

Turdidae (Thrushes)

408	Pied Thrush *Geokichla wardii*	UM
409	Orange-headed Thrush *Geokichla citrina*	SM
410	Spot-winged Thrush *Geokichla spiloptera*	E

411	Sri Lanka Scaly Thrush *Geokichla imbricata*	SE
412	Indian Blackbird *Turdus simillimus*	R
413	Eyebrowed Thrush *Turdus obscurus*	V
414	Sri Lanka Whistling-thrush *Myophonus blighi*	SE

Muscicapidae (Old World Flycatchers and Chats)

415	Rufous-tailed Scrub-robin *Cercotrichas galactotes*	V
416	Oriental Magpie-robin *Copsychus saularis*	CR
417	White-rumped Shama *Kittacincla malabarica*	R
418	Indian Black Robin *Saxicoloides fulicatus*	R
419	Asian Brown Flycatcher *Muscicapa dauurica*	M
420	Brown-breasted Flycatcher *Muscicapa muttui*	M
421	Spotted Flycatcher *Muscicapa striata*	V
422	Blue-and-White Flycatcher *Cyanoptila cyanomelana*	V
423	Dusky Blue Flycatcher *Eumyias sordidus*	UE
424	Blue-throated Flycatcher *Cyornis rubeculoides*	V
425	Tickell's Blue Flycatcher *Cyornis tickelliae*	R
426	Bluethroat *Cyanecula svecica*	V
427	Yellow-rumped Flycatcher *Ficedula zanthopygia*	V
428	Kashmir Flycatcher *Ficedula subrubra*	SM
429	Blue Rock-thrush *Monticola solitarius*	SM
430	Rufous-tailed Rock-thrush *Monticola saxatilis*	V
431	Indian Blue Robin *Luscinia brunnea*	M
432	Whinchat *Saxicola rubetra*	V
433	Siberian Stonechat *Saxicola maurus*	V
434	Pied Bushchat *Saxicola caprata*	UR
435	Pied Wheatear *Oenanthe pleschanka*	V
436	Desert Wheatear *Oenanthe deserti*	V
437	Isabelline Wheatear *Oenanthe isabellina*	V

Irenidae (Fairy-bluebirds)

438	Asian Fairy-bluebird *Irena puella*	V

Chloropseidae (Leafbirds)

439	Golden-fronted Leafbird *Chloropsis aurifrons*	UR
440	Jerdon's Leafbird *Chloropsis jerdoni*	R

Dicaeidae (Flowerpeckers)

441	Thick-billed Flowerpecker *Dicaeum agile*	UR
442	White-throated or Legge's Flowerpecker *Dicaeum vincens*	UE
443	Pale-billed Flowerpecker *Dicaeum erythrorhynchos*	CR

Nectariniidae (Sunbirds)

444	Purple-rumped Sunbird *Leptocoma zeylonica*	CR
445	Purple Sunbird *Cinnyris asiaticus*	R
446	Loten's Sunbird *Cinnyris lotenius*	R

Ploceidae (Weavers)

447	Streaked Weaver *Ploceus manyar*	UR
448	Baya Weaver *Ploceus philippinus*	R

Estrildidae (Waxbills)

449	Indian Silverbill *Euodice malabarica*	UR
450	White-rumped Munia *Lonchura striata*	R

451	Black-throated Munia *Lonchura kelaarti*	UR
452	Scaly-breasted Munia *Lonchura punctulata*	R
453	Tricoloured Munia *Lonchura malacca*	R
Passeridae (Old World Sparrows)		
454	House Sparrow *Passer domesticus*	R
455	Chestnut-shouldered Bush-sparrow *Gymnoris xanthocollis*	V
Motacillidae (Pipits and Wagtails)		
456	Forest Wagtail *Dendronanthus indicus*	M
457	White Wagtail *Motacilla alba*	SM, HSM
458	White-browed Wagtail *Motacilla maderaspatensis*	V
459	Citrine Wagtail *Motacilla citreola*	HSM
460	Western Yellow Wagtail *Motacilla flava*	M, SM, HSM
461	Grey Wagtail *Motacilla cinerea*	M
462	Richard's Pipit *Anthus richardi*	SM
463	Paddyfield Pipit *Anthus rufulus*	R
464	Tawny Pipit *Anthus campestris*	V
465	Blyth's Pipit *Anthus godlewskii*	SM
466	Olive-backed Pipit *Anthus hodgsoni*	V
467	Red-throated Pipit *Anthus cervinus*	V
Fringillidae (Finches)		
468	Common Rosefinch *Carpodacus erythrinus*	V
Emberizidae (Buntings)		
469	Black-headed Bunting *Emberiza melanocephala*	V
470	Red-headed Bunting *Emberiza bruniceps*	V
471	Grey-necked Bunting *Emberiza buchanani*	V

Key References for Checklist

del Hoyo, J. & Collar. N. (2014). *HBW and Birdlife International Illustrated Checklist of the Birds of the World*. Vol. 1: Non-passerines. Lynx Edicions, Barcelona.

del Hoyo, J. & Collar. N. (2014). *HBW and Birdlife International Illustrated Checklist of the Birds of the World* Vol. 2: Passerines. Lynx Edicions, Barcelona.

Olsen, K. M. (2018). *Gulls of the World: a Photographic Guide*. Helm Identification Guides. Christopher Helm, London.

Rasmussen, P. C. & Anderton, J. C. (2005). *Birds of South Asia: The Ripley Guide*. Vols 1 and 2. Smithsonian Institution and Lynx Edicions, Washington, DC and Barcelona.

Wijesinghe, D. P. (1994). *Checklist of the Birds of Sri Lanka*. Ceylon Bird Club Notes Special Publication Series No. 2, Ceylon Bird Club. Colombo.

Bibliography

del Hoyo, J. & Collar. N. 2014. *HBW and Birdlife International Illustrated Checklist of the Birds of the World. Volume 1: Non-passerines.* Lynx Edicions: Barcelona.

del Hoyo, J. & Collar. N. 2014. *HBW and Birdlife International Illustrated Checklist of the Birds of the World. Volume 2: Passerines.* Lynx Edicions: Barcelona.

de Silva Wijeyeratne, G. 2019. *A Photographic Field Guide to the Birds of Sri Lanka.* 2nd ed. John Beaufoy Publishing Ltd: London.

Harrison, J. 2011. *A Field Guide to the Birds of Sri Lanka.* Oxford University Press: Oxford.

Henry, G. M. 1971. *A Guide to the Birds of Ceylon.* 2nd ed. Oxford University Press: India.

Phillips, W. W. A. 1978. *Annotated Checklist of the Birds of Ceylon (Sri Lanka).* Revised ed. Wildlife and Nature Protection Society of Sri Lanka in Association with the Ceylon Bird Club: Colombo.

Rasmussen, P. C. & Anderton, J. C. 2005. *Birds of South Asia: The Ripley Guide.* Vols 1 and 2. Smithsonian Institution and Lynx Edicions: Washington, DC and Barcelona.

Svensson, L., Mullarney, K., Zetterstrom, D. & Grant, P. 2009. *Collins Bird Guide.* 2nd ed. Harper Collins Publishers: London.

Warakagoda, D., Inskipp, C., Inskipp, T., & Grimmet, R. 2012. *Birds of Sri Lanka.* Christopher Helm Publishers Ltd: London.

Wijesinghe, D. P. 1994. *Checklist of the Birds of Sri Lanka.* Ceylon Bird Club Notes Special Publication Series No. 2, Ceylon Bird Club: Colombo.

Tour Operators

In the acknowledgements, I mention Jetwing Eco Holidays, with whom I worked for many years. A non-exhaustive list of tour operators is given below, including some of the other companies who have supported my field work.

Adventure Birding www.adventurebirding.lk

Birding Sri Lanka www.birdingsrilanka.com

Bird and Wildlife Team www.birdandwildlifeteam.com

Eco Team (Mahoora Tented Safaris) www.srilankaecotourism.com

Jetwing Eco Holidays www.jetwingeco.com

Little Adventures www.littleadventuressrilanka.com

Natural World Explorer www.naturalworldexplorer.com

Nature Trails www.cinnamonnaturetrails.com

Walk with Jith www.walkwithjith.com

Organizations

The Sri Lanka Natural History Society (SLNHS) www.slnhs.lk, email: slnhs@lanka.ccom.lk.

Field Ornithology Group of Sri Lanka (FOGSL) fogsl.cmb.ac.lk/, email: fogsl@cmb.ac.lk

Ruk Rakaganno, the Tree Society of Sri Lanka rukrakaganno.wixsite.com/rukrakaganno, email: rukrakaganno09@gmail.com.

Wildlife and Nature Protection Society (WNPS) www.wnpssl.org, email: wnps@sltnet.lk.

The Young Zoologists' Association of Sri Lanka (YZA) www.yzasrilanka.lk, email: srilankayza@gmail.com.

▪ INDEX ▪

■ INDEX ■

Other guides to Sri Lankan wildlife by Gehan de Silva Wijeyeratne